sushi american style

sushi

american style

style

tracy griffith

PHOTOGRAPHS BY GINA SABATELLA

Clarkson Potter/Publishers
New York

Published by Clarkson Potter/Publishers, New York, New York.
Member of the Crown Publishing Group, a division of Random House, Inc.
www.crownpublishing.com

CLARKSON N. POTTER is a trademark and POTTER and colophon are registered trademarks of Random House, Inc.

Printed in China

Design by Jane Treuhaft
Food styling by Tracy Griffith

Library of Congress Cataloging-in-Publication Data
Griffith, Tracy.
    Sushi American style / Tracy Griffith.
1. Cookery (Fish)   2. Sushi.   I. Title.
    TX747.G828   2004
    641.6'92—dc22   2003017635

ISBN 1-4000-5103-7

10 9 8 7 6 5 4 3

First Edition

acknowledgments

To my sister, who started it all by introducing me to sushi for the very first time at a place called Something's Fishy in Malibu when I was twelve. To my father, who inspired in me a deep devotion to food and cooking. He was a loyal sushi man way back when sushi wasn't cool and he would have been very proud of this book. To my brother, who kept the recipes vibrant with his culinary panache. To my fellow sushi fanatic Wave-o, who kept me afloat in every way. To George and Albert, who got me organized and introduced me to my most ardent agent, Coleen O'Shea. To my friend and chef sensei, Jason Yamazaki, who shared his artistry and kindness and turned it all around for me. *Arigato, Jason-san.* To Gina, for her gorgeous photographs, which saved my sushi rolls. To fabulous Freddie, for the first photos.

Especially to my beautiful mother, Nanita Greene, who is the source of grace and light for me and the reason I can shine. This Catfish Roll's for you, Mama!

Finally, to the wonderful and lovely ladies of Clarkson Potter: Pam, Adina, Marysarah, Jane, Sibylle, and Linnea. A first-time author couldn't have been luckier or gotten a more patient, savvy, and enthusiastic team. Thank you for taking a chance on me, this book, and the Elvis Roll.

contents

introduction

This cookbook is going to bypass the raw-fish angst and move straight into the really fun part—making sushi.

I was working behind the counter in a trendy Beverly Hills restaurant making sushi for the beautiful people when I heard the usual *unusual* request: "I don't like raw fish. What else can you make me?" "I hate that seaweed stuff." "Ya got anything *cooked* back there?" ● I'd smile blankly, furiously thinking, *What can I make them? Why are they here? Why don't they go to Burger King?* ● And so, these ideas for unconventional sushi came out of the need to satisfy these less-than-intrepid but eager sushi eaters. A fried-chicken roll seemed beneath the art of sushi at first, but I had to admit it tasted great and customers loved it. Fascinated with the delicious possibilities of Western ingredients prepared with Japanese techniques, I started writing down these sushi American style ideas. ● It was a big change from a few months earlier, when, after a degree in theater arts and years of acting classes in New York and L.A., I was drowning in the whimsical waves of Tinseltown and desperate for some control over my creative life. The time had come for me to figure out what I really wanted. I wanted REAL again. Pure. Simple. Sushi!

There it was: the California Sushi Academy—a clean white building with clouds of white steam wafting around smiling students in chef whites, tossing gleaming white rice and rolling spicy tuna rolls. Was it heaven?

I arrived for my first day of sushi academy, ready to roll.

"STAAACY!" Stacy? I thought I was the only girl in class.

"STAAACY!!!" Oh. Someone was yelling at *me*. It was my teacher, Masa. Taut and wiry as a whippet, Masa was a master sushi chef and something of a sensation in Tokyo. Teaching a class about his sacred art to a bunch of L.A. *gaijin,* including a girl, was clearly not his life's calling. In a torrent of barely decipherable English, he let me know everything that was wrong with me: I had on nail polish, I wore my hat backwards, I had too much hair, the wrong shoes, pants too big, apron askew. I was unnatural. Hey, wait a minute. *Unnatural?*

A lot of people, sushimen (and that is what male sushi chefs are called) and customers alike, in the über-traditional world of sushi, consider it unnatural for women to be sushi chefs. They say that our hands are slightly hotter than men's, making for sticking rice and poor-tasting fish. Some believe we have inferior reflexes and, at the low end, there are still those who think we're unclean.

I laughed. This was the twenty-first century! This was L.A.! Nothing was unnatural!

For the next several months, Masa and I tangled through the course, complete with angry tears and humiliating failure. I had to admit there might be something to the hotter-hands theory. Masa said he'd never seen so much rice stick to one person in his whole life and I certainly hadn't either. I also butchered fish, sharpened knives wrong, ruined rice, wrecked pickles, and dropped the miso. But Masa kept demanding, forcing me to focus on detail, to become reverent about simplicity and the quality of ingredients. I thank him now for he is how I came to understand and love this delicate cuisine.

Freshly graduated and eager, I set out to look for a job. *Whew,* I thought, *after sushi boot camp, working at a restaurant will be a breeze!*

• • •

"Ha-ha!" the manager laughed. "Oh, no, no, no! No such thing as a sushiwoman!" He nearly rolled off his chair.

I was interviewing for a sushi chef position at an upscale sushi joint in West Hollywood. I looked at him. "I *am* a sushiwoman. I am a bona fide sushiwoman."

I whipped out my CSA certificate. He barely glanced at it.

"Nice, nice. For waitress? Hostess? Okay. But for sushiwoman?" He started to break up again. "Ha-ha. No. No."

It was pretty much the same story all over town. Sure, I had a discrimination case. What girl doesn't? But I didn't want to start off my new career under a cloud of accusations. I put the word out to people who knew people in the restaurant biz—I needed a sushi gig.

"Hey, Trace, a friend of mine is opening this place called Tsunami's . . ."

It was to be *the* hot spot in Beverly Hills, with an innovative Pan-Asian menu, a nightclub, private VIP room, and two sushi bars. Restaurateur Mark Fleischman knew a good novelty angle when he saw one—a redheaded girl sushi chef! The sushimen were appalled by my lack of experience. I was, too.

But after a while, with so much intense practice, I got the hang of it. Soon I had my own following of customers, including the "special" ones who helped me branch out with new ideas for sushi.

When most people think of sushi they think of raw fish, and when they are attempting sushi at home, they're not sure about the *raw* aspect. How do you choose and fillet a fish? Where do you even find sushi-grade quality fish? Do you have to go to a commercial fish market at 5:00 A.M., or is it safe to buy it from the grocery store? This cookbook is going to bypass the raw-fish angst (though there are a few easy raw-fish recipes included just in case you want to try them) and move straight into the fun part—making sushi.

Sushi literally means "seasoned rice." Sushi rice can be seasoned with a sweet vinegar dressing for savory rolls and with puddings or sweet syrups for desserts. So even without using raw fish, you are technically making sushi. And a few techniques are all you need to make this inventive and delightful food. After your first roll, you'll be hooked, and practice will make perfect in no time; soon you'll add sushi making to your culinary repertoire.

Most of the ingredients are familiar and easy to find. Many of the accents are Asian but well known—like soy sauce, ginger, scallions, and sesame seeds. You'll also learn how to use less common ingredients like nori, rice vinegar, mirin (sweet rice cooking wine), and wasabi. All of these are typically found in the Asian section of most supermarkets and health food stores. A sharp knife, a rice cooker, a bamboo rolling mat, and a good cutting board are the only essential tools for making sushi.

Having your ingredients prepared and ready to "roll" makes creating sushi effort-less. Plus, it's really, really fun and all your friends will be so impressed. Rock around the sushi tonight!

if you're going to use raw fish . . .

In order to be consumed raw, freshwater fish like salmon and perch must *always* be frozen before using and saltwater fish must be über-fresh and marked "sushi-grade" or "sashimi-grade" quality. This is to ensure a minimum of health risks like parasites. Your fishmonger should be able to tell you if your fish is sushi-grade quality or has been flash-frozen or FAS ("frozen at sea"). The difference in taste between fresh fish and frozen/thawed-out fish is like the difference between homegrown tomatoes and ketchup. But if you cannot find sushi-grade fish, the frozen kind is acceptable. In order to make sure your fish is fresh, gently poke the fillet to look for a springy resistance. You can also test freshness by sniffing the package; it should smell of clean seawater and should not smell fishy. (Sniffing for freshness is highly effective. Don't be embarrassed.) Also, there shouldn't be a lot of water running around the bottom of the package.

If you can't find FAS or sushi-grade quality fish, take your *very* fresh fillets home, wrap them first in plastic and then in aluminum foil, and freeze them for at least 24 hours and for up to 7 days in the coldest freezer you can find. The temperature experts recommend −4°F, but 24 hours in a standard 0–5°F freezer will do the trick.

When you are ready to use the fillets, remove the foil and thaw them in the refrigera-tor, which should take 2 to 3 hours.

getting

started

It really is as easy as set, prep, and roll. Once you've set up your basic equipment (rice cooker, cutting board, and knives), prepared your basic sushi rice, and cut your familiar ingredients into simple strips, you are ready to rock and roll. Getting down the basic setup will leave you free to create your sushi with ease and, most important, fun!

ingredients glossary

All these ingredients can be found in the Asian section of supermarkets. You can also check out websites like sushifoods.com or sushilinks.com.

Mirin A Japanese sweet cooking rice wine (actually a sake) with a sugar content of 25 percent and an alcohol content of 14 percent. It has been used for centuries to lend a subtle, mellow flavor to sauces and dressings, and to firm meats and fish during cooking. For a mirin substitute, combine one part water, one part white wine, and one part sugar.

Nori A sea plant harvested from saltwater inlets in Japan. Nori is naturally rich in vegetable protein, vitamins, and minerals, has a subtle smoky aroma, and hints at a taste of the sea. It is chopped, rolled, and dried in the sun, then toasted and packaged in crisp sheets used to make sushi rolls. The standard size is 8 x 7 inches, but it also comes in a larger 10 x 8-inch size. Look for the pre-toasted or roasted variety called yaki-nori (*yaki* means "roasted"). It's important to keep the package sealed to keep the nori dry. Close the package with tape if it doesn't have

a secure closure. If nori becomes soggy (which it does quite easily—like potato chips do), hold an edge with kitchen tongs and wave the nori briefly over an open flame.

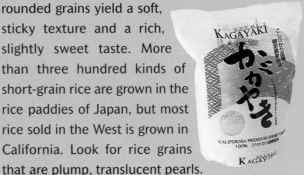

Rice The short-grain *japonica* variety is the preferred type of rice for sushi because its rounded grains yield a soft, sticky texture and a rich, slightly sweet taste. More than three hundred kinds of short-grain rice are grown in the rice paddies of Japan, but most rice sold in the West is grown in California. Look for rice grains that are plump, translucent pearls. Commonly available brands include Blue Rose, Kokuho Rose, Kagayaki Select, and Nishiki. No other type of rice can be substituted for sushi rice.

Rice vinegar A delicate and sweet Japanese vinegar perfect for adding to dressings and softening saltiness in sauces. An excellent complement to mirin, and milder than wine or apple cider vinegars, it also comes in a seasoned version with added sugar and salt, and a light seasoned version with reduced sugar and salt. It is the staple ingredient in sushi rice dressing.

Sesame seeds Available in black, brown, and white varieties. White sesame seeds are sold toasted and untoasted. You can buy pretoasted sesame seeds or toast them yourself in a dry frying pan over medium heat until they are glossy and fragrant. It is always better to lightly toast even pretoasted sesame seeds right before you use them, as it freshens their fragrance and flavor.

Sesame-salt seasoning A delicious combination of white and black sesame seeds and sea salt. If you can't find it commercially, prepare it yourself by combining ¼ cup toasted black sesame seeds, ¼ cup toasted white sesame seeds, and 1 tablespoon sea salt.

Soy sauce The indispensable Japanese seasoning sauce made by fermenting soybeans, wheat, salt, and water. It is used in almost every recipe here, and its unique saltiness and mellow sweetness is considered a most important hidden flavor. It is available in a dark version and a saltier light version. Tamari, a richer soy sauce made with no wheat and by longer fermentation, is the soy of choice for those on a wheat-free diet. Dark soy and tamari are the two types most commonly available.

Sriracha chili sauce (or Korean chili sauce) This smooth, fire-colored chili sauce has a complex, sweet, and hot flavor with a touch of garlic that is hard to substitute. The choice of many a sushi chef to add the heat to spicy tuna rolls, it has a kick, but it won't hurt you like the heat from

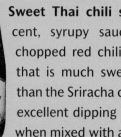

habañero peppers. It usually comes in a convenient plastic squeeze bottle. It is not to be confused with sweet Thai chili sauce (see below).

Sweet Thai chili sauce A translucent, syrupy sauce flecked with chopped red chilies and its seeds that is much sweeter and milder than the Sriracha chili sauce. It is an excellent dipping sauce by itself or when mixed with a little soy sauce.

Wasabi Though its name means "mountain hollyhock," wasabi is a wild, river-growing rhizome related to ginger and horseradish. Freshly grated wasabi has a biting, clean, peppery taste, but wasabi is rarely used in its superb natural form. It must grow in clean, running water, so it is not mass-farmed, and is very expensive. (It retails for about $100 a pound. If you want to try real wasabi—do it! Check out freshwasabi.com. They sell it by the ounce.) Commercial wasabi is usually mixed with mustard and horseradish powders, cornstarch, and food coloring, and is available as a powder in cans or as a ready-to-use paste in tubes. Though it isn't 100 percent wasabi, it still adds a unique kick to soy sauce, dressings, and mayonnaises.

equipment and utensils

You can find the following equipment and utensils in kitchenware departments of gourmet stores or department stores. Also check online stores like chefscatalog.com or cooking.com.

Knives

You'll need two sharp 6- to 7-inch knives: one for chopping, slicing, and dicing and the other for cutting sushi rolls. It is essential to have a very sharp knife to cut sushi rolls—otherwise they'll get mashed flat. If you're not sure how to sharpen it yourself, find a professional blade-sharpening person. They'll sharpen it safely (incorrect sharpening can ruin a blade), cheaply, and well. The sharpness will last a long time and—especially when it comes to sushi—you will learn that happiness is a sharp knife.

Rice Cooker

Please buy an electric rice cooker. They are inexpensive, easy to use, and yield perfect rice every single time. (Almost every household in Japan has one.) Rice cookers work at a constant temperature, spreading heat evenly around the sides and bottom. The cooker automatically turns off at the right time and can keep your sushi rice on a Warmer setting so that it will stay fresh for hours. Cold rice gets stiff, is hard to handle, and doesn't taste as good.

A 6- to 8-cup rice cooker will cost you from $25 to $40 and includes a handy rice paddle. These machines are splendid for everyday sushi rice. You can spend as much as $400 for a top-of-the-line rice cooker that can cook everything from rice to polenta to porridge.

Bamboo Rolling Mat

A rolling mat, or *makisu,* to roll sushi. Buy the 9½ x 8-inch standard size. The mat is made of bamboo sticks; one side is flat and pale green (used for rolling) and the other side is rounded and pale yellow (used for shaping). Lay the mat green-side up when rolling sushi.

Cutting Board

Besides a rice cooker, a big cutting board (get one that measures about 22 x 16 inches) is the center of your sushi world. Use one as thick and heavy as possible so it's solid enough not to move around with all the cutting and rolling going on. If it does slip about, wet a kitchen towel, wring it out, and lay it flat on the counter. Place the cutting board squarely on top to anchor it.

Freestanding Wire-Mesh Sieve

The perfect utensil for washing and drying rice, this sieve has a flat bottom and legs, so that it stands upright.

Large Flat-Bottomed Wooden or Glass Dish

The Japanese use a special tub made expressly for dressing sushi rice, but you can fake it with a big wooden bowl that is free of salad dressing residue (or else the rice will absorb the taste) or a large glass baking dish.

Squeeze Bottles

Because of their squeezability and small tip opening, these bottles give you great control for adding mayonnaises and sauces to rolls and garnishing plates. Most sauces can be kept in them for weeks.

Vegetable Peeler

Please throw away the wand-type peeler. For clean, smooth cuts, get a new, sharp, Y-shaped peeler.

Zester/Microplaner Grater

You'll need a good, sharp zester to get long curls of citrus zest for garnishes. To finely grate citrus zest and ginger, use a microplane grater. It can grate many things, including ginger, garlic, and hard cheeses.

Small Dishes for Dipping Sauces

Each person should have his or her own supply of dipping sauce, so be sure to have several dishes on hand.

sushi rice

The first and most important step in the sushi-making process is preparing the rice. If your rice is tasty, your sushi will shine. By learning these few simple steps, you will have perfect rice every time.

MAKES ABOUT 6 CUPS COOKED RICE

3 cups short-grain white sushi rice

Rice Dressing (see page 20)

1 Pour the rice into a freestanding wire-mesh sieve. Under cold tap water, gently swish the rice around with your fingers until the water runs almost clear. About a minute is enough. Do not overrinse, as this may break the grains and make the rice lose too much starch.

2 To dry, fan the rice up and around the sides of the colander, exposing the maximum surface area to air. Let the rice sit for about 30 minutes, until it is completely dry.

3 Place the rice and 3 to 3¼ cups water (see Note) in a 4- to 6-cup rice cooker and click to the Cook setting. In about 20 minutes, it will click off. Do not open the lid; let the rice rest untouched for about 15 minutes. This is the steaming time and it is essential to the rice's success. Once the rice is cooked, it is ready to be dressed.

4 With a rice paddle, scoop the rice from the cooker insert to a large shallow wooden bowl or a large glass baking dish. Set the cooking insert aside. You'll be putting the rice back into it after dressing it.

5 Spread out the hot rice with the edge of the paddle evenly over the bottom of the bowl in an angled slashing motion. Holding the paddle perpendicularly over the rice, drizzle the dressing over the back of the paddle evenly over the rice surface. With the paddle slice and fold the dressing through the rice until the grains are coated and glossy. After a little practice, you'll find your own dressing rhythm.

6 Place the dressed Sushi Rice back into the cooker and cover with a clean, damp kitchen towel to keep in the moisture. Click the cooker button onto the Warmer set-

ting. Sushi Rice is easier to handle when it's warm and it tastes better, too. Sushi Rice doesn't have to be warm when you serve it, just when you are preparing the rolls.

NOTE It is normal to have some rice stuck to the bottom of the rice cooker, and this will not affect the taste of the rice. In Japan, these crunchy bits are the children's favorite.

A note on water-to-rice ratio

Sushi rice is available in two versions: old crop and new crop. The new crop rice becomes available in the fall and will be marked as such. This rice requires less water and should be adjusted to a 1:1 ratio of water to rice. Also check cooking instructions on each bag of rice.

VARIATION

stovetop method

1 Use a heavy-bottomed 3- or 3½-quart saucepan with a tight-fitting lid. The proper size is important. The water level should not fill more than a third of the saucepan.

2 Put the washed and dried rice in the pot with 3¼ cups of water. Over high heat, bring to a boil and boil for 1 minute. Foam should bubble up around the lid, but be careful not to let the rice boil over. Reduce the heat to medium and simmer for 3 more minutes.

3 Reduce the heat to low and cook for 12 to 15 minutes. Remove from the heat and let stand, covered and undisturbed, for 15 minutes. This is the steaming portion of the cooking. Dress the rice as directed in step 5 on the opposite page.

rice dressing (SUSHI-ZU)

MAKES ½ CUP

The sweet vinegar dressing used on Sushi Rice is called sushi-zu (zu *means "vinegar") and is the secret to glossy Sushi Rice with body and sticking power. This delicate dressing can be made ahead of time and kept in the refrigerator for weeks. The taste only improves with age. About 1 generous tablespoon of dressing to 1 cup of cooked rice is a good guideline. You can adjust the sweetness of your* sushi-zu *to taste.*

½ cup rice wine vinegar
3 tablespoons sugar
1 teaspoon salt

1 In a small saucepan, stir the vinegar, sugar, and salt over low heat until the sugar and salt dissolve. Do not let the mixture boil. Or microwave for 60 seconds on High. Stir to dissolve.

2 Set aside to cool and store in a screw-top jar.

a note on getting organized

An important part of easy sushi making is having prepped, ready-to-roll ingredients and handy equipment.

Your sushi world revolves around the rice cooker holding the warm Sushi Rice. This should always be near your cutting board, on which should lay your rolling mat, knife, and a damp kitchen towel. Next to the cutting board and rice cooker, place a bowl of cold water with a splash of rice vinegar in it (use a 3:1 ratio of water to vinegar). This is what you dip your fingers in before handling Sushi Rice to prevent it from sticking to your hands. Arrange dishes of the prepared filling ingredients, nori sheets, and a few extra clean kitchen towels nearby, and you're ready to roll!

small

rolls

The key to success in rolling small rolls is thinking, well, small. Think delicate, subtle. Small rolls are less forgiving than big rolls that can take a lot of ingredients and still close. With small rolls, there isn't a lot of leeway for zealous ingredient stuffers. Use less than you might reckon, especially when you are learning. A small roll is really just a dab of rice and a few slender sticks of ingredients rolled up in a little half sheet of nori.

how to roll a small roll

1 To prepare nori, if you can't find precut nori half sheets, simply cut a whole sheet in half. First, inspect a full sheet of nori and notice the pressed lines running across the surface, then fold in half. The fold should be in the same direction as those pressed lines. You want to end up with a half sheet with a size of 4 x 7 inches. Run a knife (or cut with a scissors) along the fold to split the nori in half.

2 Prepare a finger bowl of cold water with a splash of vinegar at the ready for wetting your fingers and palms (the proportion of water to vinegar should be about 3:1). Arrange the filling ingredients in small dishes and have them, along with the half sheets of nori, handy near your cutting board and rice cooker.

3 Place the rolling mat green-side up with the slats running horizontally. Place the nori half sheet horizontally (the pressed lines in the nori running the same way as the slats in the mat) on your rolling mat, with the smoother, shinier side down. It is very important to always make sure that the edges of the mat and the nori are flush at the bottom edge nearest you or else your roll won't roll right.

4 Wet your hands in the finger bowl and scoop out about $1/3$ cup of Sushi Rice. Form it into a very loose ball about the size of a plum. Place the rice ball in the center of the nori.

5 Gently flatten the rice ball and spread the rice over the nori using the following 6-step process.

- Spread the upper-left portion of rice toward the upper-left corner of the nori (leaving a 1-inch border at the top).
- Spread the lower-left portion of rice to the lower-left corner of the nori.
- Spread the mid-top portion of rice toward the mid-top of the nori (leaving a 1-inch border at the top).
- Spread the mid-bottom portion of rice to the mid-bottom of the nori.
- Spread the upper-right portion of rice toward the upper-right corner of the nori (leaving a 1-inch border at the top).
- Spread the lower-right portion of rice to the lower-right corner of the nori. Smooth over any lumps and fill any holes. The rice layer should be 3 to 4 grains thick.

This is not as complicated as it sounds. Having this simple arrangement in your head will give you a rice-spreading rhythm in no time. (This will go nicely with your rice-dressing rhythm.)

6 The roll is now ready for ingredients. Fill as instructed in the recipe. Be sure to not overlap the filling ingredients too much in the middle, or your roll will have an unsightly bulge and will be hard to close.

7 With your thumbs, lift the nearest edges of the bamboo mat and the nori and curl up and over the ingredients that you are holding in with your fingers. Roll over until the edges of the mat and the nori touch the rice on the far side. Squeeze the length of the mat to shape and tighten the roll. Holding the mat securely around the roll with one hand, lift the edge of the mat slightly, letting it slide forward (so you don't roll the mat

troubleshooting

If a seam won't stay closed, leave the roll on the mat, gently scrape away some rice from the bottom edge, and remove some ingredients. Then wet a finger, swipe it down the length of the bottom edge of the nori seam, and reroll. You can also try cutting a repair strip of nori lengthwise into a 2-inch-wide strip. This expands the roll's girth. Wet a finger and swipe one edge of the nori repair strip to moisten it. Line it up with the bottom roll seam and slip it under (with the shiny side down and moistened edge up) so that the edges overlap by about an inch. The nori repair strip should lay flat on the mat. Now moisten the outer facing edge of the repair strip and immediately roll over to close the seam. Squeeze, and let the roll set in the mat for a minute before removing it and cutting.

into the roll), and continue rolling a half turn to completely close the roll. Now is when you can squeeze your roll into a round or square shape. Remove the roll from the mat and place it onto the cutting board.

8 Dip the point of a very sharp knife into the finger bowl and upend the knife, tapping the butt of the knife to allow water to run down the blade. Start with the knifepoint poised over the middle of the roll at a 45-degree angle. Using one flowing and sure motion, slice forward and then pull back and down smoothly. Horizontally stack the 2 half pieces side by side. Holding the roll halves together, make 2 even cuts through them into thirds or make 3 even cuts into fourths for smaller pieces. Wet and wipe the knife between cuts. (You'll get into the habit of wetting and wiping, wetting and wiping your knife. It makes the cutting clean and easy.) Serve the pieces with small dishes of dipping sauce on the side.

avocado grapefruit roll

This is a lyrical roll with unexpected pairings and soft pink and green colors. The scattering of salty almonds adds a "Hello!" to it. Don't worry about cutting the grapefruit into neat ¼-inch slices—it can be difficult to wrangle. Using ragged bits of it in a horizontal line will work fine.

MAKES 4 SMALL ROLLS

1 Place the nori, shiny-side down, on the rolling mat. Wet your hands and spread ⅓ cup of Sushi Rice evenly over the nori, leaving a 1-inch border at the top.

2 Dab 1 teaspoon Wasabi Mayonnaise in a line across the middle of the rice. Sprinkle 1 teaspoon crushed almonds across the rice surface. Place 2 avocado slices in a line across the middle of the rice. Place 3 grapefruit slices on the near side of the avocado. Place 2 pairs of cucumber sticks in line on the far side of the avocado. Season to taste with freshly ground black pepper.

3 Roll according to the Small Roll method (page 25). Repeat to form the remaining 3 rolls and serve with Ginger Soy Dipping Sauce.

SEE PHOTOGRAPH ON PAGE 30

2 cups prepared Sushi Rice (page 18)

4 half sheets nori

4 teaspoons Wasabi Mayonnaise (page 142)

4 teaspoons crushed salted and roasted almonds, peanuts, or cashews

½ avocado, peeled and cut lengthwise into ¼-inch slices

½ pink grapefruit, peeled and split lengthwise into sections and trimmed to slices of about ¼ inch

½ hothouse or English cucumber, cut into 4 x ¼-inch slices

Freshly ground black pepper

½ cup Ginger Soy Dipping Sauce (page 140)

Avocado
Grapefruit
Roll
(page 29)

Jicama
Lime
Roll

jicama lime roll

Don't let the simple ingredients—jicama, lime, cilantro, Wasabi Mayonnaise—fool you. This impeccable little roll is a powerhouse of sweet-tart, salty, crisp, and clean flavor—perfect for a summer snack with an ice-cold beer or chilled white sangria.

MAKES 6 SMALL ROLLS

6 half sheets nori

3 cups prepared Sushi Rice (page 18)

¼ cup Wasabi Mayonnaise (page 142)

1 medium jicama, cut into 4 x ¼-inch sticks

1 bunch of cilantro

1 or 2 limes, halved

2 tablespoons sea or kosher salt

½ cup Citrus Soy Dipping Sauce (page 141)

1 Place the nori sheet, shiny-side down, on the rolling mat. Wet your hands and scoop out about ⅓ cup of Sushi Rice. Spread evenly over the nori, leaving a 1-inch border at the top.

2 Squeeze or dab a thin line of Wasabi Mayonnaise in a horizontal line in the middle of the rice. Place pairs of jicama sticks end to end on top of the mayonnaise. Place 2 pairs of cilantro sprigs end to end alongside the jicama, letting the leaves overhang the sides of the roll. Sprinkle the jicama and cilantro with a generous squirt of lime juice squeezed right from the lime half. Each half will give enough juice for 2 or 3 rolls. Sprinkle the filling with a good pinch of salt.

3 Roll according to the Small Roll method (page 25).

4 Repeat to form the remaining 5 rolls. Garnish the plate with Wasabi Mayonnaise and serve with Citrus Soy Dipping Sauce.

roasted asparagus roll

My friend Zana uses goat cheese, sun-dried tomatoes, and pine nuts over pasta, which inspired this roll. The creamy goat cheese complements the rich sun-dried tomatoes, crunchy pine nuts, and delicate asparagus spears.

MAKES 6 SMALL ROLLS

24 thin (or 12 thick) asparagus spears, trimmed

2 teaspoons olive oil

Sea salt to taste

6 half sheets nori

3 cups prepared Sushi Rice (page 18)

1 (3½-ounce) package goat cheese, crumbled

6 teaspoons pine nuts, toasted

18 to 20 sun-dried tomato slices packed in oil, drained, patted dry, and slivered lengthwise

½ cup soy sauce or Balsamic Sauce (page 141)

1 Preheat the oven to 400°F. On a plate, toss the asparagus with the olive oil and salt. In a roasting pan with a rack, place the asparagus spears and roast for 8 to 10 minutes. Remove from the oven and let cool.

2 Place the nori, shiny-side down, on the rolling mat. Wet your hands and spread ⅓ cup of Sushi Rice evenly over the nori, leaving a 1-inch border at the top.

3 Spread 2 tablespoons of the goat cheese in a horizontal line across the middle of the rice. Sprinkle 1 teaspoon of the pine nuts on top of the cheese. Arrange a single layer of the tomatoes in a line over the goat cheese and nuts. Place 2 pairs of the roasted thin asparagus spears (or, if using thick asparagus, just 2 spears) end to end and heads out in a line along the nearest side of the tomatoes. Don't overlap the asparagus ends in the middle.

4 Roll according to the Small Roll method (page 25). Repeat to form the remaining 5 rolls. Serve with soy sauce or Balsamic Sauce for dipping.

a little lamb roll

There's some real culinary fusion packed into this little roll. It's a perfect way to use leftover lamb, roast pork, or baked ham. And everything tastes better with garlic mayonnaise.

MAKES 6 SMALL ROLLS

2 small garlic cloves,
 roasted

3 tablespoons mayonnaise

6 half sheets nori

3 cups prepared Sushi Rice (page 18)

3 tomatillos or 1 small green tomato,
cut crosswise into ¼-inch slices,
then slices cut in half

24 to 30 fresh mint leaves (optional)

½ pound cooked lamb, shredded or cut
into 4 x 1¼-inch strips (about 1 cup)

Freshly ground black pepper

½ cup soy sauce or Tempura
Dipping Sauce (page 140)

1 In a small bowl, mash the roasted garlic into a paste with a fork. Mix the garlic paste with the mayonnaise.

2 Place the nori, shiny-side down, on the rolling mat. Wet your hands and spread ⅓ cup of Sushi Rice evenly over the nori, leaving a 1-inch border at the top.

3 Dab 1 teaspoon of garlic mayonnaise horizontally across the middle of the rice. Place a single layer of tomatillo slices or green tomato slices over the mayonnaise. Place 4 to 5 mint leaves in a line over the tomatillos. Arrange about 3 teaspoons of shredded lamb over the mint. Season to taste with pepper.

4 Roll according to the Small Roll method (page 25). Repeat to form the remaining 5 rolls. Serve with soy sauce or Tempura Dipping Sauce.

miss piggy roll

Devastatingly delicious, this roll is sweet and peppery like its name-sake. It's a great way to use up leftover pork chops, tenderloin, or barbecue. Make sure to freshly crack the pepper as its frisky taste really makes this roll snap.

MAKES 6 SMALL ROLLS

1 tablespoon black peppercorns

6 half sheets nori

3 cups prepared Sushi Rice (page 18)

½ pound cooked pork, shredded or cut into 4 x ¼-inch strips

1 peach, pitted and cut lengthwise into ¼-inch-thick slices

3 jalapeño peppers, seeded and cut lengthwise into ¼-inch-thick strips

½ cup soy sauce or Tempura Dipping Sauce (page 140)

1 To crack the peppercorns, place them in a small plastic bag, squeeze out any air, and close. Lay the bag on top of a kitchen towel and crack the peppercorns with a meat mallet or a hammer.

2 Place the nori, shiny-side down, on the rolling mat. Wet your hands and spread ⅓ cup of Sushi Rice evenly over the nori, leaving a 1-inch border at the top.

3 Place 3 pork strips in a horizontal line across the middle of the rice. Place 3 peach slices in a line along the nearest side of the pork. Place 3 jalapeño strips alongside the peaches. Sprinkle with a hearty amount of cracked pepper.

4 Roll according to the Small Roll method (page 25). Repeat for the remaining 5 rolls. Serve with soy sauce or Tempura Dipping Sauce.

Ginger
Crab Roll
(page 38)

Seared Tuna
and Spicy
Radish Roll

seared tuna and spicy radish roll

This is a snappy roll that's sure to get your taste buds' attention. You can buy bottled hot sesame oil in the Asian section of supermarkets, or add a dash of cayenne pepper to plain sesame oil. This roll is also very good with the tuna solo.

MAKES 6 SMALL ROLLS

1 Season the tuna steaks with the salt and pepper. In a medium sauté pan, heat the oil until it ripples but is not smoking. Sear the tuna steaks for about 1½ minutes on each side for rare. Slice the tuna steaks thinly, about ¼ inch thick.

2 In a small bowl, coat the radish slices with the hot sesame oil.

3 Place the nori, shiny-side down, on the rolling mat. Wet your hands and spread ⅓ cup of Sushi Rice evenly over the nori, leaving a 1-inch border at the top.

4 Place 3 pieces of tuna in a horizontal line across the middle of the rice. Top the tuna slices with a double layer of the radish slices. Alongside the radish slices, place 5 to 6 radish sprouts on both sides of the roll, end to end, allowing the leaves to stick out of the sides of the roll.

5 Roll according to the Small Roll method (page 25). Repeat to form the remaining 5 rolls. Serve with soy sauce or Citrus Soy Dipping Sauce.

½ **pound 1-inch-thick sushi-grade ahi tuna steaks**

Kosher or sea salt and freshly ground black pepper

2 tablespoons olive oil

12 red radishes, thinly sliced, slices cut in half, plus 3 sliced for garnish

2 teaspoons hot sesame oil

6 half sheets nori

3 cups prepared Sushi Rice (page 18)

1 (4-ounce) package daikon radish or sunflower sprouts

½ **cup soy sauce or Citrus Soy Dipping Sauce (page 141)**

ginger crab roll

Any type of fresh crab will work for this lovely and elegant roll, rich with the tang of the sea and bright citrus. Serve it on the patio, Dahling, with sparkling prosecco, champagne, or iced green tea. To easily peel fresh ginger, use the inside edge of a teaspoon to scrape off the thin skin.

MAKES 6 SMALL ROLLS

1-inch knob fresh ginger, peeled and grated

4 teaspoons lime juice

½ teaspoon grated lime zest

2 teaspoons olive oil

Sea salt and freshly ground black pepper to taste

1 cup cooked fresh or canned crabmeat, drained

6 half sheets nori

3 cups prepared Sushi Rice (page 18)

English or hothouse cucumber, peeled and sliced into 4 x ¼-inch strips

3 scallions, halved lengthwise and trimmed into 4-inch strips

½ cup Citrus Soy Dipping Sauce (page 141)

1 In a small glass screw-top jar or a small bowl, squeeze the grated ginger pulp to extract the juice. Discard the pulp. Add the lime juice, zest, olive oil, and salt and pepper. Shake well or whisk. In a medium bowl, toss the crabmeat with the dressing.

2 Lay a half sheet of nori, shiny-side down, on the bamboo mat. Wet your hands and spread ⅓ cup of Sushi Rice evenly over the nori, leaving a 1-inch border at the top.

3 Arrange about 3 teaspoons of crabmeat in a horizontal line across the middle of the rice. Place 2 pairs of cucumber strips end to end along the far side of the crabmeat. Place 2 scallion strips in a line alongside the cucumber, with the green ends overhanging the sides of the roll.

4 Roll according to the Small Roll method (page 25). Repeat to form the remaining 5 rolls. Serve with Citrus Soy Dipping Sauce.

SEE PHOTOGRAPH ON PAGE 36

smoked trout and caramelized onion roll

*Smoky trout and silky sweet onions make this a sensuous roll.
You could also try it with smoked oysters or sardines
instead of trout.*

MAKES 6 SMALL ROLLS

1 Heat the oil and the butter over high heat until foaming. Add the sliced onion and brown on both sides.

2 Reduce the heat to medium-low. Gradually break up the onion rings and cook slowly for 25 to 35 minutes, until richly golden. Add the Balsamic Sauce and cook for another 10 minutes. Mix in the fresh thyme and remove from the heat.

3 Place the nori, shiny-side down, on the rolling mat. Wet your hands and spread 1/3 cup of Sushi Rice evenly over the nori, leaving a 1-inch border at the top.

4 Arrange about 3 teaspoons of the trout in a horizontal line in the middle of the rice. Arrange about 2 teaspoons of the onion in a line across the trout. Place a pair of parsley sprigs end to end next to the onion, letting the leaves overhang the sides of the roll.

5 Roll according to the Small Roll method (page 25). Repeat to form the remaining 5 rolls. Serve with soy sauce.

2 tablespoons olive oil

1 tablespoon butter

**1 medium sweet onion,
thinly sliced**

**1 tablespoon Balsamic Sauce
(page 141)**

1½ teaspoons fresh thyme leaves

6 half sheets nori

**3 cups prepared Sushi Rice
(page 18)**

**1 small package smoked trout
(about ½ pound), skinned and
loosely flaked**

1 bunch flat-leaf parsley

½ cup soy sauce

sesame spinach roll

These savory and delicate rolls can also be made as an inside-out roll (see page 66), sprinkled with black sesame seeds, so you can make a kind of checkerboard display when you serve them.

MAKES 6 SMALL ROLLS

1 (14-ounce) package spinach, washed

1 tablespoon freshly toasted sesame seeds

2 tablespoons smooth peanut butter

1 teaspoon sesame oil

2½ tablespoons mirin

1 teaspoon seasoned rice vinegar

1 teaspoon soy sauce

1 heaping teaspoon sugar

6 half sheets nori

3 cups prepared Sushi Rice (page 18)

5 tablespoons sesame-salt seasoning (page 15)

1 Steam the spinach, tightly covered, for about 2 minutes, until it is just wilted. Remove the spinach to a clean kitchen towel. Roll and squeeze the spinach into a tight cylinder to remove the water. Remove the spinach from the towel and place it in a medium mixing bowl.

2 In a dry skillet over medium heat, lightly toast the sesame seeds (even if they are already toasted) until shiny and fragrant. In a small bowl, combine the peanut butter and sesame oil, then mix in the sesame seeds. In another small bowl, combine the mirin, vinegar, soy sauce, and sugar, stirring until the sugar dissolves. Add the mirin mixture to the peanut butter mixture and whisk until smooth.

3 Toss the dressing with the spinach to coat it very lightly. If you have any dressing left over, use it as dipping sauce.

4 Place the nori, shiny-side down, on the rolling mat. Wet your hands and spread ⅓ cup of Sushi Rice evenly over the nori, leaving a 1-inch border at the top.

5 Arrange about 2 tablespoons of dressed spinach in a horizontal line across the middle of the rice.

6 Roll and cut according to the Small Roll method (page 25).

7 Sprinkle the sesame-salt seasoning onto a plate. Dip the top end of each cut sushi piece into the seasoning. Arrange on a plate with the sesame-seasoning side up.

8 Repeat to form the remaining 5 rolls. No dipping sauce is needed, but use plain soy sauce if desired or extra sesame dressing.

Green Bean
Dream
(page 45)

Crunchy
Tuna
Rolls

crunchy tuna roll

Charley Tuna never had it so good! Use this recipe or your own favorite tuna salad formula to fill up this adventurous deep-fried roll. Serve with sweet or sour pickles, chips, and iced tea. This roll also works well as a big roll (see page 48)—just double the filling amounts.

MAKES 4 TEMPURA ROLLS

1 In a medium bowl, mix together the tuna, mayonnaise, and scallions.

2 Prepare the tempura batter. Refrigerate the batter while you prepare the rolls.

3 Place the nori on the rolling mat. Wet your hands and spread about 1/3 cup Sushi Rice on the nori, leaving a 1/2-inch border at the top.

4 Arrange 1 tablespoon of tuna salad in a horizontal line across the middle of the rice. Place 2 pairs of carrot sticks in a line next to the tuna salad.

5 Prepare all 4 rolls according to the Small Roll method (page 25), but don't cut them.

1 (7-ounce) can water-packed tuna, drained

2 tablespoons Lemon Mayonnaise (page 142)

1 scallion, cut crosswise into thin rings

Basic Tempura Batter (page 44)

4 half sheets nori

2 cups prepared Sushi Rice (page 18)

1 carrot, peeled and cut into 4 x 1/4-inch sticks

5 cups canola or peanut oil, for frying

Sriracha chili sauce (optional)

1/2 cup Citrus Soy Dipping Sauce (page 141)

6 In a heavy pot, heat the oil to 350°F. Remove the batter from the refrigerator and place it near the rolls and the frying pot. Using your fingers, glide a roll through the batter, allowing a thin coating to adhere. Lift the roll with tongs, and carefully slide it into the 350°F oil. Fry for about 1 minute, 30 to 40 seconds on each side. The batter will turn a pale golden color. Using tongs, remove the roll and transfer it to a cutting board. (Do not drain it on paper towels as this makes tempura soggy.) Cut and serve them one at a time so that they are crispy and hot as you eat them.

RECIPE CONTINUES

7 Without wetting the knife, cut the roll into 6 even pieces. Hold the end of the roll with paper towels if it's too hot to handle with your fingers. Make sure the oil is back up to 350°F before frying the remaining rolls. Garnish the plate with spicy chili sauce, if you like, and serve immediately with Citrus Soy Dipping Sauce.

VARIATION Instead of coating this roll in tempura batter, fry it as an inside-out roll sprinkled with sesame-salt seasoning (page 15.) You'll get an outside layer of crispy-fried rice instead of crunchy batter.

basic tempura batter

The secret of crisp and light tempura is ice-cold batter and the correct frying temperature. Use ice water for the tempura batter and heat the cooking oil to 340°F for vegetables and 350°F for chicken and seafood. Ice water produces a slightly denser batter than sparkling water, but both work for sweet and savory tempuras as they are flavorless. Beer makes for an airy batter and adds richness to savory tempuras made with shrimp, chicken, or vegetables. Use a superfine flour like Wondra if you can. It absorbs liquids more rapidly and makes for a crunchier texture.

Using a deep-fry thermometer is a sure way of knowing when oil is at the perfect temperature for frying, but if you don't have one, you can tell when the oil is hot by placing the handle of a long wooden spoon in the oil. If tiny bubbles immediately form around the handle, the oil is ready for frying. Fry ingredients in small batches, 3 or 4 pieces at a time. Don't drain tempura pieces on paper towels, as doing so will make them soggy. It's better to remove them to a wooden cutting board. Eat tempura immediately after cooking to enjoy it while it's hot and crispy.

1 large egg
1 cup ice water, sparkling water, or very cold beer (depending on the recipe)
¾ cup all-purpose flour or Wondra
½ teaspoon baking soda

1 In a medium glass bowl, mix together the egg and water (or beer).

2 In a separate bowl, mix together the flour and baking soda. Add the flour mixture to the egg mixture, mixing very lightly. Don't worry about lumps—if you overmix it, the batter will become gluey. Place the batter in the refrigerator while preparing the rolls. If the batter gets too thick, add a couple of ice cubes to thin it.

green bean dream

*This roll features shapely, crunchy beans supported by rumpled radicchio and a
touch of sweet Thai chili sauce. You can also serve it with the hot Sriracha
sauce for the heat-seeking crowd. Work quickly to rock and roll
these tempura beans while they're crispy hot.*

MAKES 4 TEMPURA ROLLS

5 cups peanut or
canola oil, for frying

Basic Tempura Batter
(opposite) mixed with
2 tablespoons sesame seeds

½ pound green beans,
trimmed (4 beans per roll)

4 half sheets nori

2 cups prepared Sushi Rice (page 18)

4 teaspoons Thai sweet chili sauce

½ head radicchio, shredded,
or small beet leaves

⅔ cup Tempura Dipping Sauce
(page 140) mixed with
¼ teaspoon wasabi paste
(optional)

1 In a heavy pot, heat the oil to 340°F.

2 Meanwhile, make the tempura batter. Coat about
10 beans at a time in batter. When the oil is ready,
drop in the beans, one at a time, so they won't stick
in a clump. Fry 10 to 12 at a time, turning once, until
the beans turn golden, about 1½ minutes. Using
tongs, transfer the beans to a wooden cutting board.

3 Place the nori on the rolling mat. Wet your hands and
spread ⅓ cup Sushi Rice evenly over the nori, leaving a
½-inch border at the top.

4 Dab a thin line of chili sauce in a horizontal line across the middle of the rice. Scatter about 1 tablespoon shredded radicchio in a line
across the chili sauce, allowing the ends to overhang the side of the nori. Place
2 pairs of beans end to end in a line across the sauce, allowing the ends to overhang
the side of the nori.

5 Roll according to the Small Roll method (page 25). Repeat to make the remaining
3 rolls. Serve with Tempura Dipping Sauce.

SEE PHOTOGRAPH ON PAGE 42

big

rolls

Big rolls are the Whoppers of the sushi world. These guys can hold more than double the filling that small rolls can handle, and in three different styles. One way is by using a whole sheet of nori; another is by using a half sheet of nori turned vertically. The big roll can be rolled up in a spiral fashion as well (see page 70).

how to roll a big roll

USING A WHOLE SHEET OF NORI

1 Prepare a finger bowl of cold water with a splash of vinegar at the ready for wetting your fingers and palms (the proportion of water to vinegar should be about 3:1). Arrange the filling ingredients in small dishes and have them with sheets of nori near your cutting board and rice cooker.

2 Place a whole nori sheet, shiny-side down, on your rolling mat with the shorter 7-inch edge of the nori flush with the nearest bottom edge of the mat. The pressed lines in the nori should be horizontal, running the same way as the slats of the mat.

3 Wet your hands in the finger bowl and scoop out 1 cup of Sushi Rice. Form it into a very loose ball about the size of a peach. Place the rice ball in the center of the nori.

4 Gently flatten the rice ball and spread the rice over the nori, using the following 6-step process.

• Spread the upper-left portion of rice toward the upper-left corner of the nori (leaving a 1-inch border at the top).

- Spread the lower-left portion of rice to the lower-left corner of the nori.
- Spread the mid-top portion of rice toward the mid-top of the nori (leaving a 1-inch border at the top).
- Spread the mid-bottom portion of rice to the mid-bottom of the nori.
- Spread the upper-right portion of rice toward the upper-right corner of the nori (leaving a 1-inch border at the top).
- Spread the lower-right portion of rice to the lower-right corner of the nori. The rice layer should be even and 3 to 4 grains thick.

5 Fill roll as instructed in the recipe. Be sure not to overlap the filling ingredients too much in the middle, otherwise your roll will have an unsightly bulge and be hard to close.

6 With your thumbs, lift the nearest edge of the bamboo mat and curl it up and over the ingredients that you are holding in with your fingers. Roll over until the edge of the mat and the nori touch the rice on the far side. Squeeze the length of the mat to shape and tighten the roll. Holding the mat securely around the roll with one hand, lift the edge of the mat slightly, letting it slide forward (so you don't roll the mat into the roll) and continue rolling a half turn to completely close the roll. Squeeze the length of the mat again. Now is when you can squeeze your roll into a

RECIPE CONTINUES

round or square shape. Remove the roll from the mat and place it onto the cutting board.

7 Dip the point of a very sharp knife into the finger bowl and upend the knife, tapping the butt of the knife to allow water to run down the blade. Start with the knifepoint poised over the middle of the roll at a 45-degree angle. Using one sure motion, slice forward to three quarters up the blade and then pull back and down smoothly. Horizontally stack the two half pieces side by side. Holding the roll halves together, make 2 even cuts into thirds or make 3 even cuts into fourths. Wet and wipe the knife between cuts. (You'll get into the habit of repeatedly wetting and wiping your knife. It makes the cutting clean and easy.) Serve pieces with small dishes of dipping sauce on the side.

Note on cutting big rolls

Some people find big roll sushi that has been cut into 6 pieces just too darn big to eat. If you and/or your guests agree, be sure to cut your rolls into 8 pieces total.

how to roll **a big roll**

USING A HALF SHEET OF NORI

1 To prepare nori, if you can't find precut nori half sheets, take a full sheet and notice the pressed lines running across the surface, then fold in half. The fold should be in the same direction as the pressed lines. You want to end up with a half sheet sized 4 x 7 inches. Run a knife (or cut with a scissors) along the seam to split the nori in half.

2 Follow "Using a whole sheet of nori" steps as described on page 48, except for step 2, *vertically* place a half sheet of nori, shiny-side down, on the rolling mat. Make sure the nearest bottom edges of the mat and the nori are flush. In step 3, you will scoop out a heaping ½ cup of rice instead of 1 cup.

3 Wet the knife and cut the roll into 4 (not 6) even pieces.

catfish roll

A sushi twist and roll on an old Cajun favorite—the po'boy. Crunchy catfish sparked by crisp celery and carrot makes this one jamboree of a roll. Also try it with cornmeal-fried shrimp instead of catfish and serve with plenty of hot sauce, pickled jalapeños, and cold beer.

4 (8-ounce) catfish fillets

Sea or kosher salt and freshly ground black pepper

¾ cup buttermilk

1 egg

¾ cup white cornmeal

1 teaspoon garlic powder

¼ teaspoon cayenne pepper

2 tablespoons peanut or canola oil

4 whole sheets nori

4 cups prepared Sushi Rice (page 18)

¼ cup Spicy Mayonnaise (page 142)

½ cup grated carrot

½ cup grated celery

4 jalapeño peppers, seeded and sliced lengthwise into thin strips (optional)

4 scallions, split lengthwise

1 bunch of cilantro

½ cup Jalapeño Soy Dipping Sauce (page 140) or Citrus Soy Dipping Sauce (page 141)

Hot pepper sauce, for serving

MAKES 4 BIG ROLLS

1 Rinse the catfish fillets in cold water. Pat the fillets dry and season them with salt and pepper. In a mixing bowl, beat the buttermilk and egg together. Add the fish fillets and let them soak for 20 to 30 minutes.

2 On a large plate, spread the cornmeal, then season with 2 teaspoons salt, 2 teaspoons pepper, the garlic powder, and cayenne.

3 In a large skillet, heat the oil over medium heat. Meanwhile, dredge the fillets through the seasoned cornmeal. Fry the fish for about 3 minutes on each side, until golden brown. Remove from the skillet and drain the fillets on paper towels. Cut the fillets into halves lengthwise.

4 Place the nori sheet on the rolling mat. Wet your hands and spread about 1 cup of Sushi Rice evenly over the nori, leaving a 1-inch border at the top.

5 Dab 1 tablespoon of the Spicy Mayonnaise in a horizontal line across the middle of the rice. Place 2 fillet halves end to end across the mayonnaise. Place about 2 table-

spoons each of grated carrot and celery across the fillets. Place a few of the jalapeño strips, if using, in a line on top if you'd like. Place the scallion halves in a line next to the other fillings, letting the ends protrude out of the sides. Lay 2 bunches of cilantro, 3 to 4 sprigs each, end to end in a line across the other fillings, letting the leaves protrude out of the sides.

6 Roll according to the "Using a whole sheet" Big Roll method (page 48). Repeat to form the remaining 3 rolls. Serve with Jalapeño Soy Dipping Sauce or Citrus Soy Dipping Sauce and hot sauce.

pork chop roll

Served with a warm soup and a nice merlot, this hearty roll is the ticket for a chilly night. It's also a knockout with honey-baked ham. Mmmm!

MAKES 4 BIG ROLLS

2 tablespoons lime juice

2 teaspoons grated ginger

1 garlic clove, minced

1 tablespoon honey

½ cup apple juice

2 (4-ounce) thick-cut pork chops

Sea salt and freshly ground black pepper

½ pound butternut squash, peeled, seeded, and quartered

2 tablespoons olive oil

4 whole sheets nori

4 cups prepared Sushi Rice (page 18)

1 head endive, cut lengthwise into eighths

½ cup Balsamic Sauce (page 141) or Ginger Soy Dipping Sauce (page 140)

1 Heat the oven to 400°F.

2 In a glass baking dish, combine the lime juice, ginger, garlic, honey, and apple juice. Season the pork chops with salt and pepper and add to the marinade. Cover and marinate the chops, refrigerated, for about 30 minutes, turning once.

3 Meanwhile, in a glass baking dish, toss the squash quarters with 1 tablespoon of the olive oil and a sprinkle of salt. Bake for 15 to 20 minutes. Remove from the oven and let cool. Slice the squash into 4 x ½-inch sticks.

4 Heat the grill or grill pan to medium-high. Grill the chops for 5 to 6 minutes per side. Remove from the grill and let cool. Remove the bone and slice the chops into strips of about 4 x ½ inches.

5 Place the nori, shiny-side down, on the rolling mat. Wet your hands and spread about 1 cup of Sushi Rice evenly over the nori, leaving a 1-inch border at the top.

6 Place 2 pairs of pork slices in a line across the middle of the rice. Place 2 pairs of squash strips next to the pork. Place 2 lengths of endive next to the squash.

7 Roll according to the "Using a whole sheet" Big Roll method (page 48). Repeat to form the remaining 3 rolls. Serve with Balsamic Sauce or Ginger Soy Dipping Sauce.

thanksgiving roll

This is a new and fun way to use turkey leftovers (or rotisserie chicken). These Thanksgiving flavors, including sweet cranberry and crunchy celery, are a pleasing treat when rolled with Sushi Rice. You can make this roll even bigger with a whole sheet of nori and double the fillings.

MAKES 4 BIG ROLLS

4 half sheets nori

3 cups prepared Sushi Rice (page 18)

4 tablespoons cranberry relish or jelly

8 teaspoons mayonnaise

2 cups roasted turkey or chicken, shredded

2 celery ribs, cut into 4 x ¼-inch strips

2 scallions, split lengthwise

Soy sauce for dipping (optional)

1 Place the nori vertically on the rolling mat. Wet your hands and spread about a heaping ½ cup Sushi Rice evenly over the nori, leaving a 1-inch border at the top.

2 Spread 1 tablespoon of cranberry relish in a line across the middle of the rice. Dab 2 teaspoons of mayonnaise in a line next to the relish. Arrange about ½ cup of turkey over the mayo and relish.

3 Place 2 pairs of celery sticks in a line on the far side of the turkey. Place 2 scallion halves end to end next to the celery.

4 Roll according to the "Using a half sheet" Big Roll method (page 51). Cut into 4 even pieces. Serve with soy sauce, if you like.

two tiger roll

This roll is so "phat" it has two different sauces—one tangy green and the other smoky red. Very good versions of salsa verde, or tomatillo salsa, and chipotle sauce are found in the Hispanic section of supermarkets. Tiger shrimp are slightly smaller than colossal shrimp, and you can fit three to a roll depending on their size. If you use three tigers, cut the middle shrimp in half and arrange it so it fills out the center of the roll evenly.

MAKES 4 BIG ROLLS

12 tiger or 8 colossal-size shrimp, peeled and deveined

3 tablespoons vegetable oil

Sea salt and freshly ground black pepper

4 half sheets nori

3 cups prepared Sushi Rice (page 18)

1 small husked tomatillo or green tomato, thinly sliced

1 small red tomato, thinly sliced

1 medium avocado, peeled, pitted, and cut lengthwise into ¼-inch slices

1 bunch of cilantro

4 tablespoons prepared salsa verde or tomatillo salsa

4 tablespoons prepared chipotle sauce

½ cup Citrus Soy Dipping Sauce (page 141)

1 Soak 12 or 8 wooden skewers in water for 10 minutes.

2 With the soaked skewers, skewer the shrimp from tail to head along the belly. Heat grill or grill pan to medium. Lightly coat the shrimp with the oil, then season to taste with salt and pepper. Grill the shrimp for about 1½ minutes on each side, until opaque. Let the shrimp cool slightly, then twist and remove the skewer.

3 Vertically place the nori on the rolling mat. Spread about a heaping ½ cup of Sushi Rice over the nori, leaving a 1-inch border at the top.

4 For 2 of the rolls, arrange the tomatillo slices in a horizontal line across the middle of the rice. For the other 2 rolls, arrange the red tomato slices in a horizontal line across the middle of the rice.

5 Then, for all 4 rolls, arrange 3 tiger or 2 colossal shrimp head to head in a horizontal line across the middle of the rice, allowing the tails to protrude from the sides of the roll. Place 2 slices of avocado alongside the shrimp in each roll. Place 2 pairs of cilantro sprigs end to end, with the leaves protruding from the sides of the roll.

6 Roll according to the "Using a half sheet" Big Roll method (page 51). Repeat to form the remaining 3 rolls. Serve the rolls with small dishes of salsa verde, chipotle sauce, and Citrus Soy Dipping Sauce.

green eggs and ham roll

You don't need a "goat on a boat" to love these green eggs and ham. It makes a wonderful breakfast or brunch treat, delicious with a glass of fresh O.J.

MAKES 2 BIG ROLLS

2 large eggs

1 teaspoon lemon-pepper seasoning

¼ cup grated sharp Cheddar cheese

¼ cup mixed freshly chopped parsley, cilantro, and basil

2 teaspoons butter

2 whole sheets nori

2 cups prepared Sushi Rice (page 18)

4 thin ham slices

½ pound cooked green beans, straight and long, ends trimmed

½ cup Citrus Soy Dipping Sauce (page 141), Lemon Mayonnaise (page 142), or ketchup

1 In a glass mixing bowl, beat the eggs with the lemon-pepper seasoning until they are light yellow. Mix in the cheese and herbs.

2 In a skillet, heat the butter over medium-low heat until it is foaming. Add the egg mixture. Let the eggs set for a minute or so before loosening the bottom with a spatula. Keep the curds large by folding over the eggs, omelet style, rather than stirring them. When the eggs are done, slide them onto a cutting board and let cool.

3 Place the nori sheet, shiny-side down, on the rolling mat. Wet your hands and spread about 1 cup of Sushi Rice evenly over the nori, leaving a 1-inch border at the top.

4 Arrange 2 ham slices over the rice. Trim the slices so that they don't overlap and they cover the rice surface except for a bare inch of rice at the bottom. Place half of the eggs in a horizontal line across the middle of the ham. (Reserve the other half of the eggs for the second roll.) Place 3 pairs of green beans in a line along the far side of the eggs.

5 Roll according to the "Using a whole sheet" Big Roll method (page 48). Repeat to form the remaining roll. Serve with your choice of Citrus Soy Dipping Sauce, Lemon Mayonnaise, ketchup, or salsa.

cordon bleu roll

A French twist on a sushi roll, this jaunty number is best served with Balsamic Sauce, which complements the ham and tames the chives.

MAKES 4 BIG ROLLS

2 tablespoons olive oil

1½ pounds boneless chicken breasts (about 2 medium breast halves)

Sea or kosher salt and freshly ground black pepper

4 thin premium ham slices

8 thin slices Swiss cheese

4 half sheets nori

3 cups prepared Sushi Rice (page 18)

1 bunch of fresh chives, trimmed

½ cup Balsamic Sauce (page 141) or soy sauce

1 In a large skillet, heat the oil over medium heat. Season the chicken breasts with the salt and pepper. Sauté the chicken breasts for 3 to 4 minutes on each side, depending on the thickness. For the last 2 minutes of cooking on the second side, top each chicken breast with 1 piece of ham and 2 slices of cheese and cover. Remove the chicken from the skillet to a cutting board. While the chicken is still warm, cut each piece lengthwise into about 6 even strips.

2 Vertically place the nori, shiny-side down, on the rolling mat. Wet your hands and spread a heaping ½ cup of Sushi Rice evenly over the nori, leaving a 1-inch border at the top.

3 Place 2 or 3 strips of the chicken, ham, and cheese in a horizontal line across the lower third of the rice. Don't overlap the strips too much in the middle. Season with freshly ground black pepper. Place 2 bundles of chives, each with 8 to 10 sprigs, end to end along the farthest side of the chicken. Let the chive tops spring out of the ends of the roll by 2 to 3 inches.

4 Roll according to the "Using a half sheet" Big Roll method (page 51). Repeat to form the remaining 3 rolls. Serve with Balsamic Sauce or soy sauce for dipping.

dixie–chicken roll

This isn't your mama's fried chicken, but she'll still love this roll, filled with zesty marinated chicken, the sweet bite of onion, and your favorite coleslaw. It's an excellent roll to serve at your next picnic or hootenanny.

MAKES 4 BIG TEMPURA ROLLS

3 cups buttermilk

2 tablespoons bottled hot pepper sauce

2 chicken breast halves, cut lengthwise into 1-inch strips (about 8 strips)

2 cups all-purpose flour

2 teaspoons baking soda

2 teaspoons sea salt

2 teaspoons freshly ground black pepper

2 teaspoons garlic powder

5 cups peanut or canola oil, for frying

Basic Tempura Batter (page 44)

4 cups prepared Sushi Rice (page 18)

4 whole sheets nori

½ cup Lemon Mayonnaise (page 142)

½ cup coleslaw

1 sweet onion, cut into ¼-inch-thick slices and then halved

½ cup Citrus Soy Dipping Sauce (page 141)

Bottled hot pepper sauce, for serving (optional)

1 In a large bowl, mix the buttermilk and hot pepper sauce to make a marinade. Add the chicken strips to the marinade and coat well. Cover the bowl with plastic wrap and let the chicken marinate for several hours and up to 1 day in the refrigerator. Allow the chicken to come to room temperature before frying.

2 Mix the flour, baking powder, and seasonings in a large plastic or brown bag. In a large, deep pot, heat the oil to 365°F. Make the tempura batter. Drop the chicken strips into the flour mixture and shake the bag to coat. Dip 2 or 3 pieces of the marinated, floured chicken into the tempura batter. Fry in small batches for about 3 minutes, until pale golden brown. Remove the chicken to a wooden cutting board.

3 Spread 1 cup of Sushi Rice over a sheet of nori, leaving a 1-inch border at the top. Dab a line of 1 teaspoon Lemon Mayonnaise down the center of the rice, add 2 tablespoons coleslaw, 2 chicken strips, and a few half onion rings. Roll according to the "Using a whole sheet" Big Roll method (page 48). Repeat to form the remaining 3 rolls. Serve with the remaining Lemon Mayonnaise or Citrus Soy Dipping Sauce and bottled hot pepper sauce, if you like.

inside-out

rolls

These flipped-out rolls are fun to make and even more fun to present. They are very impressive with their white rice jackets decked out with herbs, pepper, nuts, or seeds and make a snappy change from the plain nori-wrapped rolls. And they're so versatile. They can be rolled as small rolls, big rolls, or spiral rolls.

how to roll an inside-out roll

1 Have whole and half sheets of nori ready. Have a finger bowl of cold water with a splash of vinegar (3:1 water to vinegar) at the ready for wetting your hands. Arrange the filling ingredients in small dishes and keep them and the sheets of nori handy near your cutting board and rice cooker.

2 To prevent outside rice from sticking, you'll need to cover your mat in plastic wrap. Pull out about 2 feet of plastic wrap and wrangle it flat onto the counter. Center the rolling mat, green side *down,* on top of the wrap. Holding the mat firmly, fold the left side of the wrap over the mat and smooth it toward the center. Hold it taut while you fold over the right side of the wrap to overlap with the left side seam and smooth the seam. Fold over the top and bottom edges and smooth the seams.

3 Place a whole or half sheet of nori on the wrapped mat, depending on the recipe. Wet your fingers with vinegar-water and scoop out about 1/2 cup of Sushi Rice for small rolls or 1 heaping cup of Sushi Rice for big rolls. Form the rice into a soft ball and place it in the center of the nori. Spread the rice evenly over the entire surface of the nori, using the 6-step method, but do not leave a 1-inch border.

- Spread the upper-left portion of rice to the upper-left corner of the nori.
- Spread the lower-left portion of rice to the lower-left corner of the nori.
- Spread the mid-top portion of rice to the mid-top of the nori.
- Spread the mid-bottom portion of the rice to the mid-bottom of the nori.
- Spread the upper-right portion of rice to the upper-right corner of the nori.
- Spread the lower-right portion of rice to the lower-right corner of the nori. Smooth over any lumps and fill any holes. The rice layer should be 3 to 4 grains thick.

4 If the recipe calls for sesame seeds, minced herbs, or peppercorns, sprinkle them over the rice now. Lift the nori by the upper corners and flip it over, making sure to situate the bottom edge of the rice-covered nori flush with the bottom edge of the mat.

5 Place the ingredients in a horizontal line in the middle of the nori.

6 Lift the mat and nori edges together and roll them up and over the ingredients. Roll the mat

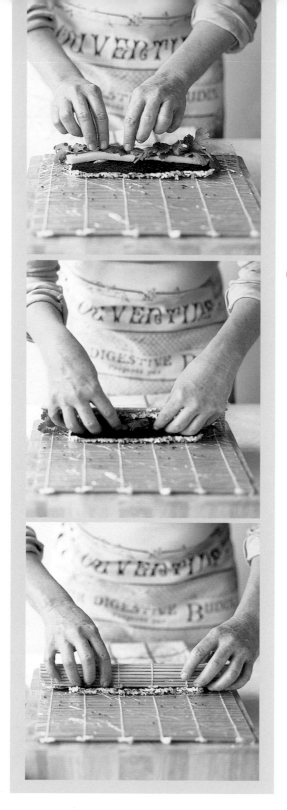

and nori over and forward until the edges come to rest on the far side of the rice bottom. Gently so you don't crush the rice grains, squeeze along the entire mat into the desired round or square shape. Lift the edge of the mat and let it slide forward as you make a half turn and squeeze again to shape and close the roll.

7 Wet your knife and cut the roll in half, then cut the halves into thirds for 6 even pieces or into fourths for 8 smaller pieces. Be sure to wipe and wet your knife after every cut.

A note on inside-out rolls

When flipping over the rice-covered nori, don't be afraid. The rice will hold and the nori shouldn't rip. Also remember that you cover the entire surface of the nori with rice when making an inside-out roll, leaving no borders. This means you can fit a couple more sticks of yummy ingredients in the filling.

how to roll an inside-out spiral roll

USING A WHOLE OR HALF SHEET OF NORI

This spiral technique produces a truly unique and attractive roll. The method is best suited for flat ingredients, like cheese slices and cold cuts.

1 Cover a whole sheet or nori with 1 cup of Sushi Rice, *or* cover a vertical half sheet of nori with ½ cup Sushi Rice, leaving a 1-inch border on the bottom only.

2 Flip the nori, keeping the border at the bottom, and layer the ingredients flush with the bottom edge of the nori, leaving a 1-inch border at the top.

3 To roll, use the mat or your fingers to curl the nearest edge of the nori into a tight spiral, as if you are rolling up a sleeping bag. Continue rolling forward until the roll is closed. Squeeze the length of the roll with the mat into a round shape.

green goddess roll

An exultation of vegetables, wrapped in a swath of creamy dressing—this is one vibrant veggie roll, both to see and to taste. And when was the last time you made delicious and easy Green Goddess dressing? It's truly divine.

MAKES 4 BIG INSIDE-OUT ROLLS

4 whole sheets nori

5 cups prepared Sushi Rice (page 18)

4 tablespoons minced fresh parsley

½ cup Green Goddess Dressing (recipe follows)

16 thin asparagus stalks, blanched (or 8 regular asparagus stalks)

1 avocado, peeled, pitted, and cut lengthwise into 12 (¼-inch-thick) strips

1 hothouse or English cucumber, peeled, seeded, and cut into 4 x ¼-inch strips

4 scallions, cut lengthwise into 4-inch strips

1 bunch of arugula

1 bunch of mint

1 bunch of basil

1 bunch of chives

½ cup Citrus Soy Dipping Sauce (page 141)

1 Cover the rolling mat with plastic wrap (see page 66). Place the nori on the rolling mat with the 7-inch side at the bottom. Wet your hands and spread about 1 heaping cup Sushi Rice evenly over the nori.

2 Sprinkle 1 tablespoon parsley evenly over the rice. Flip the nori sheet over according to the Inside-Out method (page 66).

3 Dab 3 level teaspoons of Green Goddess Dressing in a horizontal line across the center of the nori.

4 Over the dressing, arrange 2 pairs of thin asparagus spears end to end, letting the tips of the spears stick out of the sides of the nori. Arrange 3 pieces of avocado in a line alongside the asparagus. Lay 2 pairs of cucumber strips end to end alongside the avocado. Place 2 scallion strips end to end alongside the cucumbers. Place 3 pairs of arugula leaves in a line next to the scallions. Place 3 pairs of mint leaves in a line over the arugula. Place 3 pairs of basil leaves in a line alongside the mint. Place 2 bunches of chives, each with 6 to 8 sprigs, in line next to the basil.

5 Roll according to the Inside-Out method. Repeat to form the remaining 3 rolls. Serve with Citrus Soy Dipping Sauce.

Green
Goddess
Roll

Sesame Shrimp
and Mango Roll
(page 74)

green goddess dressing

MAKES 1 CUP

2 to 3 anchovy fillets, rinsed and patted dry (optional)

2 tablespoons chopped parsley leaves

1 teaspoon chopped tarragon leaves

1 teaspoon chopped basil leaves

1 small garlic clove, mashed with coarse salt to a paste

3 tablespoons sour cream

¾ cup mayonnaise

1 teaspoon fresh lemon juice

Sea salt and freshly ground black pepper to taste

Place all the dressing ingredients in a blender and puree until smooth. The dressing will keep for
3 to 4 days in the refrigerator.

sesame shrimp and mango roll

Tender shrimp and silky mango are an irresistible combination for this bespeckled inside-out roll. Serve with a simple green salad and fresh lime margaritas.

MAKES 4 SMALL INSIDE-OUT ROLLS

12 large shrimp, peeled and deveined

2 teaspoons canola or peanut oil

5 tablespoons sesame-salt seasoning (see page 15)

4 half sheets nori

2 cups prepared Sushi Rice (page 18)

2 teaspoons black sesame seeds

1 large mango, peeled, pitted, and sliced into 4 x ¼-inch strips (see Note)

4 scallions, split lengthwise

1 bunch of cilantro

1 package edible flowers for garnish (optional)

2 limes, quartered

½ cup Jalapeño Soy Dipping Sauce (page 140) or Ginger Soy Dipping Sauce (page 140)

1 Soak 12 wooden skewers in water for 10 minutes.

2 Preheat the oven to 450°F.

3 Take each shrimp and thread a wooden skewer through the belly, from the head to the tail. This will prevent curling. Lightly coat the shrimp with oil. On a large plate, spread 4 tablespoons of the sesame-salt seasoning. Press both sides of shrimp into the sesame-salt seasoning, coating well.

4 Arrange the shrimp in a single layer in a shallow baking pan and bake for 2 minutes. Turn over and bake for 2 minutes more, until they are just opaque. Remove the shrimp from the oven and let cool slightly before removing the skewers.

5 Cover the rolling mat with plastic wrap (see page 66). Lay a sheet of nori on the plastic wrap.

6 Spread about ½ cup Sushi Rice evenly over the entire nori sheet. Lightly sprinkle the surface of the rice with a few pinches of black sesame seeds. Flip the nori over according to the Inside-Out method (page 66).

7 Place 3 pieces of shrimp end to end, in a horizontal line across the center of the nori. Tuck 2 pairs of mango slices end to end alongside the shrimp. Place a pair of scallion

sprigs alongside the mango. Lay 2 pairs of cilantro sprigs alongside the scallions, allowing the leafy ends to overhang the sides of the nori.

8 Roll according to the Inside-Out method (page 66). Arrange pieces on a plate with edible flowers, if using, and lime quarters. Serve with Jalapeño Soy Dipping Sauce or Ginger Soy Dipping Sauce.

NOTE For the mango slices, cut the flat sides lengthwise, through the skin. Then just trim away the skin from each slice.

Green Goddess
Roll
(page 72)

Sesame
Shrimp and
Mango Roll

club roll

Try all kinds of cold cut combos with this pinwheeling roll—ham, smoked chicken, pastrami, bologna. Make sure you use thin slices of meats and cheese. If you can't find thinly sliced prepackaged cold cuts, ask your deli people to cut them for you. Remember to cover the nori with the Sushi Rice, leaving a 1-inch border at the bottom, then flip it over and leave a 1-inch border at the top when you layer in the fillings. This is a great sushi platter for children or the Monday night football gathering. Serve it with soda, beer, potato chips, and pickles.

MAKES 4 BIG INSIDE-OUT SPIRAL ROLLS

4 half sheets nori

2 cups prepared Sushi Rice (page 18)

6 to 8 large green leaf lettuce leaves, trimmed to fit roll

8 thin, 5 x 4-inch jack, Cheddar, or American cheese slices (about 8 ounces)

24 thin, 2-inch salami rounds (5 to 6 ounces)

8 wafer-thin sweet onion slices, broken into rings (about 1 small)

12 to 16 wafer-thin tomato slices (about 1 medium)

Freshly ground black pepper to taste

8 thin, 5 x 4-inch turkey slices (about 8 ounces)

½ cup soy sauce (optional)

Choice of mustard, mayonnaise, ketchup, pickles, for serving

1 Place the nori vertically on the rolling mat. Wet your hands and spread about ½ cup of Sushi Rice evenly over the nori, leaving a 1-inch border at the bottom. Take the nori and flip it over, keeping the border edge at the bottom.

2 For each roll, arrange a single layer of lettuce leaves flush with the bottom edge of the nori. Leave a 1-inch border at the top. Vertically place 2 trimmed slices of cheese over the lettuce. Arrange about 6 slices of salami over the cheese. Arrange a few rings of onion over the salami. Arrange 3 to 4 trimmed tomato slices evenly over the onions. Season the tomatoes with pepper. Vertically place 2 slices of turkey over the tomatoes.

3 Roll according to the Inside-Out method for spiral rolls (page 70). Repeat to form the remaining 3 rolls. Serve with soy sauce for dipping, if desired, and dishes of mustard, mayo, ketchup, pickles, and relish as condiments.

upbeet roll

This earthy roll uses very small beet leaves. If you can't find them, use mâche or any other baby red lettuce leaves (there is a prepackaged red leaf lettuce mélange available) like red chard, red mustard, or red romaine; or just use some of the left-over fresh, raw radicchio.

MAKES 4 SMALL INSIDE-OUT ROLLS

½ **pound fresh beets with tops, scrubbed and dried**

Lemon-pepper seasoning to taste

1 small head radicchio

1 tablespoon olive oil

4 half sheets nori

2 cups prepared Sushi Rice (page 18)

4 teaspoons sesame-salt seasoning (page 15)

16 to 18 small beet leaves from beets

½ **cup Jalapeño Soy Dipping Sauce (page 140), Ginger Soy Dipping Sauce (page 140), or Citrus Soy Dipping Sauce (page 141)**

1 Preheat the oven to 400°F.

2 Trim the leaves from the beets and reserve several of the smaller, prettier leaves. Cut the beets in half and place in a glass mixing bowl. Toss with some of the lemon-pepper seasoning.

3 Slice the radicchio crosswise into ½-inch slices. Brush the slices lightly with some of the oil. Season one side of the slices with lemon-pepper seasoning. Place the beets and radicchio in 1 or 2 large baking dishes or a heavy ovenproof skillet. Roast the vegetables for about 20 to 25 minutes, stirring the beets and turning the radicchio slices once, until the edges of the beets and radicchio are browned.

4 Remove the vegetables from the oven and let cool. Cut the beets and radicchio lengthwise into ½-inch strips. In a large bowl, mix them together and check the seasoning.

5 Cover the rolling mat with plastic wrap (see page 66).

6 Place the nori on the rolling mat. Wet your hands and spread about ½ cup Sushi Rice evenly over the nori. Sprinkle the rice with about 1 teaspoon sesame-salt seasoning. Flip the nori sheet over according to the Inside-Out method (page 66).

7 Place 3 to 4 teaspoons chopped beets and radicchio in a horizontal line across the middle of the nori. Place a few reserved little beet leaves in a line next to the beets, allowing the leaves to overhang the sides of the nori.

8 Roll according to the Inside-Out method (page 66). Repeat to form the remaining 3 rolls. Serve with Jalapeño Soy Dipping Sauce, Ginger Soy Dipping Sauce, or Citrus Soy Dipping Sauce.

cowboy roll

This big American steak roll will magnificently exhibit your sushi showmanship and give your guests a wild taste for more succulent steak and craggy blue cheese surrounded by plucky pink peppercorns.

MAKES 4 BIG INSIDE-OUT ROLLS

2 tablespoons coarsely cracked black pepper

1 tablespoon coarse sea or kosher salt

2 pounds (1-inch-thick) beef tenderloin, London broil, or chuck steak

2 tablespoons vegetable oil

4 whole sheets nori

4 cups prepared Sushi Rice (page 18)

2 tablespoons coarsely cracked pink peppercorns

½ cup Wasabi Mayonnaise (page 142)

½ cup crumbled Maytag blue, Gorgonzola, or Saga Blue cheese

½ red onion, cut into ¼-inch rings, rings cut in half

1 bunch of arugula or baby spinach

½ cup Jalapeño Soy Dipping Sauce (page 140)

1 Spread the black pepper and salt onto a plate and press both sides of the fillet into the seasonings to coat.

2 Heat the oil in a grill pan over high heat. Reduce the heat to medium and cook the fillet 8 to 10 minutes on each side for medium rare. Let the tenderloin rest for 10 minutes. Slice the tenderloin into ¼-inch-thick slices.

3 Wrap the rolling mat with plastic wrap (see page 66).

4 Place the nori on the rolling mat. Wet your hands and spread about 1 cup Sushi Rice evenly over the nori. Sprinkle the surface of the rice with about 1 teaspoon pink peppercorns. Flip the nori sheet over according to the Inside-Out method (page 66).

5 Dab about 3 teaspoons of the Wasabi Mayonnaise in a horizontal line across the middle of the nori. Place 4 to 6 slices of tenderloin in a line on top of the mayonnaise. Sprinkle about 3 tablespoons blue cheese alongside the beef. Break up 2 half onion rings in a line over the cheese, letting the ends overhang the edge of the roll. Place several arugula or baby spinach leaves in a line over the onions.

6 Roll according to the Inside-Out method (page 66). Repeat to form the remaining 3 rolls. Serve with Jalapeño Soy Dipping Sauce.

hand

rolls

Hand rolls are like Hollywood starlets: They're up for a good party anytime, they get along famously with everybody, and they are never spotted wearing something less than smashing. The other great thing about hand rolls is that they deliver instant gratification. Roll. Eat. Yum. No knife work involved. And nobody doesn't like to roll these sassy little numbers. Rolling them in a cone style is easy and rolling them in a cylinder style is even easier. Success lies in using small amounts (less than the amount used in a small roll) of filling ingredients and letting your imagination roll!

how to roll hand rolls

All hand rolls use half sheets of nori. If you can't find precut nori half sheets, simply cut a whole sheet in half.

FOR THE CONE HAND ROLL

1 Inspect a full sheet of nori and notice the pressed lines running across the surface, then fold in half. The fold should be in the middle and in the same direction as those pressed lines. You want to end up with a half-sheet size of 4 x 7 inches. Run a knife (or cut with a scissors) along the fold to split the nori into a proper half. Stack these half sheets like cards and place on a plate.

2 Before you roll, have a finger bowl with a splash of vinegar and a clean, damp kitchen towel standing by.

3 Take a half sheet of nori and lay it, shiny-side down, horizontally in the palm of your left hand. Wet your fingers and the palm of your right hand in the finger bowl. Scoop out about 2 tablespoons Sushi Rice and roll around in your right palm to form a loose oblong shape. This will take some practice. Gently press (rather than spread) the rice oblong down the left side of the nori.

4 If you use sauce or mayonnaise, dab a thin line down the middle of the rice. Holding the nori almost flat in your left palm, place 1 to 2 strips of each ingredient in a vertical line up the middle of the rice, letting the tops extend out of the top of the roll. Less is better: you don't need as much rice or filling as you think.

5 Now shift your hands and hold the nori between both palms like a book. Anchoring the roll with your right hand, push up the lower-left corner of the nori with your left thumb toward the top-middle edge. Curl the corner over and tuck it under the ingredients. Continue curling up in a spiral motion to form a cone shape.

6 Seal the corner of the nori with a couple of mashed grains of rice.

serving hand rolls

Serve hand rolls wrapped with colorful cocktail napkins, colored cellophane, or paper cones. Place wrapped rolls in champagne flutes or shot glasses or lay them sideways, alternating heads and tails, on a platter.

PHOTOGRAPHS CONTINUE

hand rolls **85**

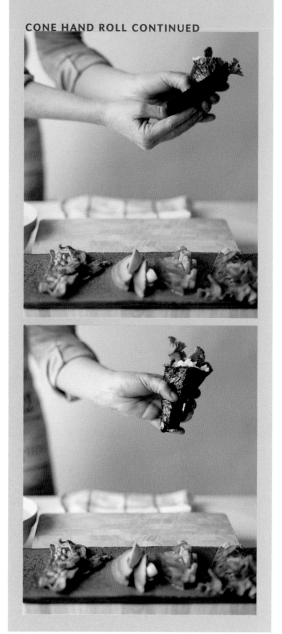

FOR THE CYLINDER HAND ROLL

1 Follow steps 1 and 2 on page 84.

2 Horizontally place the nori, shiny-side down, on a work surface.

3 Wet your fingers and the palm of your right hand in the finger bowl and scoop out about 2 tablespoons Sushi Rice. Form it into a loose oblong shape and press the rice oblong into the left side of the nori.

4 If you use sauce or mayonnaise, dab a thin line down the middle of the rice. Place 1 or 2 strips of 2 or 3 ingredients in a horizontal line on the near side of the rice, letting the tops extend out of the top of the roll. Again, less is better: you don't need as much rice or filling as you think.

5 Holding the ingredients in with your fingers, roll them up like a poster into a cylinder shape. Seal the edge by moistening with a wet finger.

rocket roll

The peppery salad green we call arugula is known as rocket *in England. Crispy, pepper-spiked chicken, with a tangy jalapeño-lime-soy sauce, makes this an extra jet-packed roll.*

MAKES 6 TO 8 TEMPURA HAND ROLLS

FOR THE MARINADE

4 scallions, chopped

2-inch knob peeled fresh ginger, grated

¼ teaspoon crushed red pepper flakes

1 jalapeño, seeded and coarsely chopped

¼ cup lime juice

½ cup soy sauce

¼ cup olive oil

2 chicken breast halves, cut lengthwise into ½-inch strips

5 cups canola or peanut oil, for frying

Basic Tempura Batter (page 44)

4 teaspoons cracked black pepper

6 to 8 half sheets nori

1 cup prepared Sushi Rice (page 18)

½ cup Lemon Mayonnaise (page 142)

1 bunch of arugula

½ cup Citrus Soy Dipping Sauce (page 141)

1 In a glass bowl, combine the marinade ingredients. Place the chicken strips in a shallow glass dish and pour the marinade over the chicken. Cover and refrigerate for several hours or overnight.

2 When the chicken has marinated, remove from the refrigerator and let it reach room temperature.

3 In a heavy pot, heat the 5 cups of oil to 350°F. Meanwhile, prepare the tempura batter, adding the cracked black pepper to the batter.

4 Allowing bits of the marinade to stick to the chicken strips, dip the chicken into the tempura batter and fry 2 or 3 pieces at a time. Remove to a cutting board.

5 Roll each roll according to the Hand Roll method (page 84): Press 2 tablespoons of rice into the left side of the nori. Use a teaspoon of Lemon Mayonnaise, 1 chicken strip, and 2 to 3 arugula leaves per roll. Serve with Citrus Soy Dipping Sauce.

VARIATION Instead of tempura frying, marinate and grill whole chicken breasts, then cut them into strips before using them in the filling.

Rich and
Famous
Roll
(page 90)

BLT
Hand Roll

blt hand roll

Supremely juicy, this roll makes its own dipping sauce and lives up to its namesake's reputation as a superbly satisfying lunch.

MAKES 6 TO 8 HAND ROLLS

1 Fry the bacon and drain on paper towels. Cut the bacon into 4 x ½-inch strips.

2 Following the Hand Roll method (page 84) for each roll, press 2 tablespoons of rice into the left side of the nori. Dab a thin line of Wasabi Mayonnaise down the center of the rice. Lay in or 2 bacon strips, 1 tomato slice, 1 avocado slice, and a few lettuce leaves. Season to taste with freshly ground black pepper.

10 bacon strips

1 cup prepared Sushi Rice (page 18)

6 to 8 half sheets nori

½ cup Wasabi Mayonnaise (page 142)

1 tomato, cut lengthwise into ½-inch-thick strips

1 avocado, cut lengthwise into ¼-inch strips

1 cup mixed baby lettuces

Freshly ground black pepper

rich and famous roll

Go ahead! Indulge yourself with a luxury ingredient, lobster. This roll is a new twist on the sushi-lovers' favorite, the California roll. It's a spectacular-looking roll, with whole lobster claws topped with little jewels of salmon roe, but it is just as tasty if you use tail meat and mayonnaise.

MAKES 4 HAND ROLLS

5 cups canola or peanut oil, for frying

Basic Tempura Batter (page 44)

1 cup (about ½ pound) cooked lobster meat, including 2 whole claws, and tail meat cut lengthwise into ½-inch-thick strips

½ cup prepared Sushi Rice (page 18)

4 half sheets nori

2 teaspoons Wasabi Mayonnaise (page 142)

1 cup mixed baby lettuce leaves

1 avocado, peeled and cut lengthwise into ¼-inch-thick slices

2 teaspoons salmon roe (optional)

½ cup Tempura Dipping Sauce (page 140) or Citrus Soy Dipping Sauce (page 141)

1 In a large heavy pot, heat the oil to 350°F. In a large bowl, make the tempura batter.

2 Glide the lobster meat through the batter to coat lightly, and fry quickly for 45 seconds to 1 minute—just until the batter turns lightly golden. Remove the lobster to a work surface.

3 Roll each roll according to the Hand Roll method (page 66). Press 2 tablespoons of rice into the left side of the nori. Dab a thin line of Wasabi Mayonnaise vertically in the middle of the rice. Lay a pair of baby lettuce leaves vertically next to the mayonnaise, letting the leaves protrude out of the top. Place 1 avocado slice in a line next to the lettuce. Use a whole claw each for 2 of the rolls and strips of tail meat for the remaining 2 rolls.

4 Top each roll with ½ teaspoon salmon roe, if you like. Serve with Tempura Dipping Sauce or Citrus Soy Dipping Sauce.

party rolls

Hand rolls are great fun for parties–it's easy and fun to let guests "roll their own."

First, prepare enough Sushi Rice for your number of guests. Figure about ⅛ cup (2 tablespoons) of rice for each roll and average 4 or 5 rolls per person. This works out to ½ of cup rice per guest. However, adjust your reckoning depending on whether the party rolls are for appetizers or dinner.

Keep the rice cooker on the Warmer setting, covered with a clean, damp kitchen towel, and place it near the ingredients and right next to the stacks of nori. Set out a buffet line of small dishes and glasses of ingredients cut into strips about 4 x ¼ inches. Firm strips of ingredients like celery, cucumber, carrot, and jicama can be placed sprouting out of assorted beverage glasses. So can sprigs of herbs like scallion, chives, cilantro, and so on. Tempura-fried ingredients are good, but only if you fry and serve them immediately, which might be something you don't want to be stuck in the kitchen doing. It's better to offer fried items fried in a light dusting of cornmeal or flour so they won't get soggy. Think of ingredients that will taste good at room temperature. Fresh herbs, lettuces, and vegetables can rest on plates placed on a larger platter of crushed ice. Large ice-filled bowls can hold smaller bowls offering perishable ingredients like tuna and egg salad, coleslaw, and cheeses. Be sure to coat apples and avocados with fresh lemon juice to avoid browning. Set out sauces and mayonnaises in bottles and spice shakers.

Offer finger bowls filled with a 3:1 solution of water to vinegar and a damp hand towel for each guest.

As the fabulous host, demonstrate the hand roll technique to your guests according to the Hand Roll method (page 84). Then offer lots of encouragement and sake and let them roll!

Here's a list of possible ingredients for you to choose from:

MEATS Grilled steak, chicken, sausage, pulled pork, bacon, prosciutto, ham, roast beef, meatloaf, turkey, bologna, salami, pastrami, fried chicken

FISH Catfish, soft-shell crab or shrimp, anchovies (fresh or canned), sardines, smoked salmon, oysters or trout, cooked shrimp, crabmeat or lobster, tunafish salad

COOKED VEGETABLES Grilled peppers, leeks, scallions, marinated peppers, pickles, sautéed collard greens, spinach, bok choy, green beans, mushrooms, asparagus, roasted squash, leeks, sweet potatoes

RAW VEGETABLES Avocado, tomato, scallion, radicchio, baby lettuces

SPRIGS OF FRESH HERBS cilantro, chives, parsley

SAUCES AND SPICES Assorted flavored soy sauces (see pages 140–141), mayonnaises (see page 142), and spices like sesame salt, black pepper, and red pepper flakes.

fancy

sushi

Just when you thought you'd seen sushi rolled every which way, here are some other fun ways to style your sushi to give it a chic flair. Learn to use canapé cutters and cookie cutters to mold rice into fanciful shapes that are a delightful change to rolls. They can be offered as party snacks or individual appetizers. ● Next, discover that sushi doesn't always have to come rolled in a nori wrapper. Here's sushi for the "I can't eat seaweed" crowd, wrapped in lettuce or rice paper, prosciutto or roast beef. Finally, sushi in bowls relieves any rice-forming stress. See how to artfully arrange your ingredients over steaming rice for the well-dressed sushi bowl.

"watermelon" sushi

*At first glance, your guests won't know if this is a slice of fruit or a sushi delight.
The spicy-hot tuna contrasts nicely with the cool cucumber. You can control
the heat by adjusting the amount of chili sauce in the Spicy Mayo.*

**1 unpeeled hothouse or
English cucumber at least
1½-inches in diameter and
cut crosswise into 10- to
12½-inch-thick rounds**

**¾ cup minced sushi-grade ahi
tuna**

**2 teaspoons Spicy Mayonnaise
(page 142)**

**½ cup prepared Sushi Rice
(page 18)**

**1 teaspoon black sesame
seeds**

**½ cup Citrus Soy Dipping
Sauce (page 141)**

MAKES 10 TO 12 PIECES

1 Using a 1½-inch-round canapé cutter with a scalloped
edge, cut the center of the cucumber out and reserve the
centers for garnish. In a small glass mixing bowl, mix the
tuna with the mayonnaise. Firmly press 1 teaspoon of
rice into each cucumber circle to fill it halfway.

2 Top the rice with about 1 teaspoon of the spicy tuna. Top
the tuna with a few scattered black sesame seeds to resem-
ble watermelon seeds. Serve with Citrus Soy Dipping Sauce.

deviled eggs

Sunny yellow bundles are topped with delicious dots of sparkling salmon-colored pearls or spiky green chives.

MAKES 10 PIECES

1 In a small glass bowl, combine the eggs, mayonnaise, and lemon-pepper seasoning.

2 Grease the inside of a 2-inch-round or -square smooth-edged canapé or cookie cutter very, very lightly with an oil-coated piece of paper towel. Dip the cutter in a small bowl of water and shake off the excess. Wipe the cutting board with a damp kitchen towel and set the cutter on the damp surface. Wet your hands and firmly press about 2 teaspoons rice into the cutter to fill it halfway. Remove the rice piece from the cutter.

3 Take a nori strip and wrap it around the rice piece, making sure the bottom edge of the nori is flush wih the bottom edge of the rice. Dampen the end of the strip to seal. Top the rice with a dollop of the egg mixture, filling to the top of the nori strip. Repeat to make 9 more pieces. Top half the pieces with a few salmon caviar eggs and the other half of the pieces with the chives.

4 Serve with soy sauce or Citrus Soy Dipping Sauce.

3 hard-boiled eggs, peeled and finely chopped

4 teaspoons Lemon Mayonnaise (page 142)

½ teaspoon lemon-pepper seasoning

½ cup prepared Sushi Rice (page 18)

1¼ sheets nori, cut into 10 (7 x 1-inch) strips (use scissors)

3 tablespoons salmon caviar

2 tablespoons fresh chives, snipped into 1-inch pieces

½ cup soy sauce or Citrus Soy Dipping Sauce (page 141)

VARIATION Instead of salmon caviar, top the eggs with a dot of thick tomato salsa or a sprinkle of sesame-salt seasoning (page 15).

coleen's canapés

Sparkling, seared scallops, wrapped in tailored nori vests and crowned with citrus zest, stand tall in their exquisite attendance. This recipe's named for my agent, Coleen, a scallop queen.

MAKES 10 PIECES

¼ fresh orange juice

2 tablespoons white miso paste

1 teaspoon white wine

2 teaspoons fresh lime juice

1 teaspoon sesame oil

1 orange

1 scallion, cut into 2-inch matchsticks

4 teaspoons peanut oil

10 medium sea scallops

Sea salt and freshly ground black pepper

½ cup prepared Sushi Rice (page 18)

1¼ sheets nori, cut into 10 (7 x 1-inch) strips (use scissors)

Sriracha chili paste (optional)

½ cup soy sauce or Citrus Soy Dipping Sauce (page 141)

1 In a small bowl, whisk together the orange juice, miso, wine, lime juice, and sesame oil. Cover and set aside.

2 Use a sharp zester to zest about ¼ of the orange. Try to get long, thin curls. In a small bowl, put the orange zest and scallion matchsticks into ice water to curl them. Pat dry before using as a garnish.

3 In a skillet or a grill pan over medium-high heat, heat the peanut oil. Season both sides of the scallops with salt and pepper. When the oil ripples, sear the scallops on each side for about 2 minutes. Remove the scallops to a platter and spoon ½ teaspoon of the orange-miso sauce over each warm scallop. Set aside, reserving the extra sauce for later use.

4 Grease the inside of a 1½-inch-round smooth-edge canapé cutter very lightly with an oil-coated piece of paper towel. Dip the cutter in a small bowl of water and shake off the excess. Wipe the cutting board with a damp kitchen towel and set the cutter on the damp surface (this will prevent the rice from sticking to the cutting board). Wet your hands and firmly press about 2 teaspoons of rice into the cutter to fill it halfway. Slide the rice piece out of the cutter and top with a scallop.

5 Take a nori strip and wrap it around the scallop and rice piece like a belt. Dampen the end of the nori strip to seal. With scissors, cut off the nori end at an angle. Top each scallop with a dot of chili paste, if you want spicy, and a curl each of orange zest and scallion. Repeat with the rest of the ingredients to make 10 pieces. Serve with soy sauce or Citrus Soy Dipping Sauce.

sushi shish kabobs

These little bites will amuse the mouth and whet the appetite while offering an array of ingredients. Fun to assemble and serve, they will brighten any sushi party.

MAKES 18 PIECES

6 cooked medium shrimp, cut into 2-inch squares

6 cilantro leaves

1 very thin lemon slice, cut into 8 wedges

2 cups prepared Sushi Rice (page 18)

1 roasted red pepper, cut into 12 (1 x ¼-inch) strips

6 prosciutto slices, trimmed into 2-inch squares

6 smoked salmon slices, trimmed into 2-inch squares

10 whole chives, blanched

Jalapeño Soy Dipping Sauce (page 140) or Citrus Soy Dipping Sauce (page 141)

1 Soak 6 (7-inch) wooden skewers in water for 10 minutes.

2 Cut the shrimp along the back almost through. Butterfly the shrimp out on a cutting board and gently tap with the back of a knife to flatten out the shrimp body.

3 Lay a 12-inch-square piece of plastic wrap on the work surface. In the center of the plastic wrap, place 1 cilantro leaf. On top of the cilantro, place 1 lemon wedge. Place 1 piece of the shrimp, back-side down, on top of the lemon.

4 Wet your hands and scoop out a walnut-sized ball of Sushi Rice. Lay the rice ball on top of the shrimp. Gather up the 4 corners of the plastic wrap and twist the rice ball until the wrap tightens; squeeze a few seconds and release. Remove the rice ball from the plastic wrap.

5 Skewer the shrimp/cilantro ball and slide to the end of the skewer, leaving a 2-inch space for the handle.

6 Lay a 12-inch-square piece of plastic wrap on the work surface. Place 2 crossed strips of red pepper on the plastic wrap. Center the prosciutto over the red pepper.

7 Wet your hands and scoop out a walnut-sized ball of Sushi Rice. Lay the rice ball on top of the prosciutto. Gather up the corners of the plastic wrap and twist close around the rice ball, squeezing for a few seconds. Remove the rice ball from the plastic wrap.

8 Skewer the prosciutto ball next to the shrimp kabob.

9 Lay a 12-inch-square piece of plastic wrap on the work surface. Center a piece of salmon on the wrap. Place a rice ball on top of the salmon. Gather up the corners of the plastic wrap and twist around the rice ball, squeezing gently. Remove the rice ball from the plastic wrap.

10 Wrap a string of chive around the salmon ball. This can be a wee challenge, so it's a good thing you have extra. Skewer the salmon ball next to the prosciutto ball.

11 Place all the skewers on a large serving platter with small dishes of Jalapeño Soy Dipping Sauce or Citrus Soy Dipping Sauce.

VARIATIONS Try wrapping the rice balls with any of these combinations or your own creations:

• Marinated red or yellow peppers topped with a tiny curl of anchovy and a shred of basil

• Avocado slice with a wafer-thin lemon wedge tied with a string of blanched chive

• Prosciutto with a sliver of honeydew melon

• Pastrami, a strip of provolone, and sweet pickle

• Before twisting up the rice balls in plastic wrap, lightly sprinkle some of them with black or white sesame seeds, almonds, crushed pink peppercorns, or dried herbs.

the mushroom guys

These rakish guys have a lot of personality to go with their earthy flavors and stylin' figures.

1 tablespoon sesame seeds, plus ½ teaspoon for garnish

1 cup prepared Sushi Rice (page 18)

¼ cup mirin (see page 14)

3 tablespoons soy sauce

10 medium shiitake or cremini mushroom caps, stemmed

1 tablespoon canola oil

Parsley leaves, for garnish

½ cup Tempura Dipping Sauce (page 140)

MAKES 10 PIECES

1 In a small skillet, toast the sesame seeds (even if they are toasted, toast them again to get a fresher flavor) over low heat until they are shiny and golden. Crush the sesame seeds with a mortar and pestle or in the bottom of a coffee cup with a wooden spoon. Mix the crushed seeds into the warm Sushi Rice right after dressing it. Return the mixture to the rice cooker and click on the Warmer setting.

2 In a large glass mixing bowl, combine the mirin, soy sauce, and 1 tablespoon of water. Add the mushroom caps to the mirin mixture and gently coat them. Marinate the caps for about 5 minutes.

3 Heat the oil in a skillet or grill pan over medium-high heat. Sear the marinated caps upside down for 2 minutes. Turn the caps over and grill for 1 more minute on the other side.

4 Wet your hands and scoop out about 1 heaping tablespoon of sesame rice. Press into a rice ball and set a mushroom cap on top. Fit the rice ball size to the cap size accordingly. Sprinkle the top of the cap with a pinch of sesame seeds. Continue with the rest of the rice and mushroom caps.

5 Garnish the plate with parsley leaves and serve with Tempura Dipping Sauce.

manhattan wrap

Made with lemon-accented Sushi Rice, this beautiful roll is a silky feast. The name is a nod to that American-style sushi classic, the Manhattan Roll, filled with smoked salmon and cream cheese and inspired by the classic New York bagel combination. See how we're all connected?

MAKES 4 WRAPPED ROLLS

1 Cover the rolling mat with plastic wrap (see page 66).

2 After dressing the rice as usual, fold in the lemon juice, lemon zest, and sesame seeds.

3 Using a sharp vegetable peeler, make lengthwise slices of cucumber, pulling the peeler down one side of the cucumber and then the other. Each long slice should have a little green edge on its side. (See photo on page 105.) Cut the long slices in half lengthwise. Cut the halved slices crosswise into 2-inch strips. Slice the flat sides of the mango lengthwise into ¼-inch-thick slices. Cut away the peel and trim the slices into 2-inch-long strips.

2 cups prepared Sushi Rice (page 18)

5 teaspoons fresh lemon juice

1 teaspoon grated lemon zest

2 tablespoons black sesame seeds

1 hothouse or English cucumber, halved lengthwise

1 mango

8 ounces smoked salmon, cut into 2 x ¼-inch strips

½ cup Citrus Soy Dipping Sauce (page 141)

4 Wet your hands and form about ½ cup Sushi Rice into a loose cylinder shape. Lay the cylinder in the middle of the rolling mat and pick the mat up by the top and bottom edges. The rice cylinder should lay in the middle of the mat like it's in a hammock. Holding both sides of the mat close together, shimmy the sides up and down, rolling the rice in the crease. This will form the rice into a neat cylinder, about 1 inch in diameter. Remove the rice cylinder from the mat and set on a cutting board swiped with a damp, clean kitchen towel.

RECIPE CONTINUES

5 Place alternating strips of salmon, cucumber, and mango angled vertically and side by side centered down the length of the rice cylinder.

6 Tear a piece of plastic wrap big enough to cover the roll. Take the rolling mat, yellow side facing down, and drape it over the roll, slats running vertically. Gently squeeze the length of the roll to shape and tighten the ingredient strips around the roll. Remove the mat.

7 Wet a knife and cut clean through the plastic wrap into 6 even pieces. Slowly lift the plastic wrap from the roll. Repeat to form the remaining 3 rolls.

8 Serve with Citrus Soy Dipping Sauce.

barber pole sushi

Whirling with "barber pole" stripes of flavor, this roll still tastes fine without the anchovies if you're not a fan of those wee fish. Just substitute with more mozzarella.

MAKES 4 WRAPPED ROLLS

2 cups prepared Sushi Rice (page 18)

1 roasted red bell pepper, cut into 2 x ¼-inch strips

1 roasted yellow pepper, cut into 2 x ¼-inch strips

16 to 20 medium basil leaves

4 to 6 ounces mozzarella cheese, thinly sliced into 2 x ¼-inch strips

1 can anchovy fillets, drained, patted dry, and trimmed to 2-inch strips (optional)

½ cup soy sauce or Balsamic Sauce (page 141)

1 Cover the mat with plastic wrap (see page 66).

2 Wet your hands and form about ½ cup Sushi Rice into a loose cylinder shape.

3 Lay the cylinder in the middle of the rolling mat and pick the mat up by the top and bottom edges. The rice cylinder should lay in the middle of the mat like it's in a hammock.

4 Holding both sides of the mat close together, shimmy the sides up and down, rolling the rice in the crease. This will form the rice into a neat cylinder about 1 inch in diameter. Remove the rice cylinder from the mat and set on a cutting board swiped with a damp, clean kitchen towel.

5 Place alternating strips of peppers, basil leaves, mozzarella, and anchovies, angled vertically and side by side, centered down the length of the rice cylinder.

6 Tear a piece of plastic wrap big enough to cover the roll. Take the rolling mat, yellow side facing down, and gently squeeze the length of the roll to shape and tighten it.

7 Wet a knife and cut clean through the plastic wrap into 6 even pieces. Slowly lift the plastic wrap from the roll. Repeat to form the remaining 3 rolls. Serve with soy sauce or Balsamic Sauce for dipping.

three-alarm snapper

Here's a sushi wrap for the seriously intrepid "hot" lover, featuring the mystically fiery habañero chile pepper. This sushi is still delicious when made with milder peppers like jalapeño or serrano for those who like it less hot. Remember to freeze the fish for 24 hours and thaw it in the refrigerator for 2 to 3 hours before you use it.

MAKES 4 SUSHI WRAPS

1 In a small bowl, whisk together the habañero, citrus juices, chili sauce, olive oil, and salt and pepper.

2 Put the strips of scallion and zest in a bowl of ice water to curl. Pat dry before using as a garnish.

3 Cut the fillets into small cubes, about ½-inch dice. In a glass mixing bowl, toss the fish with the habañero mixture. Let the mixture sit for about 20 minutes, stirring occasionally.

4 Add the grapefruit and herbs to the fish mixture. Use a large, wet serving spoon to scoop out about ⅓ cup rice. Wet your hands and press the rice into a spoon to form a loose oval. Place the rice in the middle of a lettuce leaf. Top the rice with 2 tablespoons of the fish mixture. Garnish each wrap with curls of scallion and zest. Repeat to form the remaining 3 wraps. Serve with Citrus Soy Dipping Sauce.

½ **habañero chile, seeded and finely chopped (wear gloves when handling)**

Juice of 1 lime

2 tablespoons grapefruit juice

½ **teaspoon Sriracha chili sauce**

1 tablespoon olive oil

Sea salt and freshly ground black pepper to taste

1 scallion, cut lengthwise into matchsticks

Zest curls of ½ lime

¼ **pound very fresh red snapper or perch fillets, frozen and thawed (see page 11)**

2 grapefruit segments, roughly chopped

2 basil leaves, finely chopped

2 mint leaves, finely chopped

1½ **cups prepared Sushi Rice (page 18)**

4 large butter or green leaf lettuce leaves

½ **cup Citrus Soy Dipping Sauce (page 141)**

roast beef with frizzled leeks and carrots

This roll has a real rock-and-roll style, exploding with wild-looking garnishes. It sports an unusual roast beef wrapper and a surprise creamy center.

MAKES 4 WRAPPED ROLLS

2 cups canola or peanut oil, for frying

½ carrot, cut in half lengthwise

½ small leek or scallion, sliced into 3 x ¼-inch strips

4 teaspoons prepared horseradish sauce

3 teaspoons whipped cream cheese

16 thin roast beef slices

2 cups prepared Sushi Rice (page 18)

4 thin sweet onion slices

½ cup Tempura Dipping Sauce (page 140)

1 In a heavy-bottomed saucepan, heat the canola oil to 340°F. Meanwhile, using a sharp vegetable peeler, hold the carrot half, cut-side up, firmly on the cutting board. Rake the peeler from the top to the bottom of the carrot to create long, unbroken strands. Stack 10 peels at a time and cut them lengthwise into ¼-inch strips. Fry the carrot strips for 30 to 40 seconds. Remove with a slotted spoon or wire-mesh scoop and drain on paper towels.

2 Repeat the above steps with the leek.

3 In a small bowl, mix the horseradish and cream cheese together. Set aside.

4 Cover the rolling mat with plastic wrap (see page 66). On the rolling mat, arrange 2 vertical, side-by-side, double-layer slices of roast beef to get an approximate 4 x 7-inch square.

5 Wet your hands and spread ½ cup Sushi Rice evenly over the roast beef, leaving a 1-inch border at the top.

6 Dab a heaping teaspoon of the horseradish–cream cheese mixture in a horizontal line down the middle of the rice. Place a few rings of onion in a line over the cream cheese.

7 Roll according to the Small Roll method (page 25). Top each piece with leeks or carrots. Repeat to form the remaining 3 rolls. Serve with Tempura Dipping Sauce.

rooster roll

This sushi roll comes in a calypso color burst of taste that nearly crows with excitement. Handling the delicate rice wrappers may take a little practice, so be sure to have extra sheets on hand. Use double sheets of wrappers and enjoy more success. These rolls are also quite tasty without any rice—perfect for the low-carb crowd.

MAKES 4 WRAPPED ROLLS

8 or more medium square rice wrappers

2 cups prepared Sushi Rice (page 18)

1 cup (about $\frac{1}{2}$ pound) shredded barbecued chicken

4 scallions, split lengthwise

$\frac{1}{2}$ yellow bell pepper, sliced lengthwise

$\frac{1}{2}$ red bell pepper, sliced lengthwise

1 bunch of cilantro

$\frac{3}{4}$ cup bottled sweet Thai chili sauce

1 In a large skillet big enough to hold the wrappers flat, keep 3 cups of water warm on very low heat as you work. Submerge 2 wrappers together in hot water and let them soak for about 1 minute, until the edges begin to curl and the wrappers are soft and pliable. Remove the now-stuck-nicely-together wrappers and lay them flat on a wooden cutting board. Do not pat dry.

2 Wet your hands and scoop out about $\frac{1}{2}$ cup Sushi Rice. Carefully spread the rice evenly over the wrappers, leaving a 2-inch border at the top. Place about $\frac{1}{4}$ cup chicken in a horizontal line across the middle of the rice. Place 2 scallion halves in a line beside the chicken. Place 2 each of yellow and red pepper strips in a line alongside the scallions. Place several cilantro sprigs end to end alongside the peppers, with the leaves overhanging the sides of the wrappers.

3 Roll up with your hands, without a rolling mat, like a sushi roll—holding in the ingredients and rolling snugly. Be careful not to tear the wrapper. Cut the wraps into 4 even pieces. Repeat to form the remaining 3 wraps. Serve with sweet Thai chili sauce for dipping.

prosciutto wrap

This glamorous roll, with its combination of succulently ripe pear and soft Gorgonzola, will melt in your mouth. Make sure to use thin prosciutto for this wrap.

MAKES 4 WRAPPED ROLLS

16 thin prosciutto slices

2 cups prepared Sushi Rice (page 18)

1/2 cup crumbled Gorgonzola cheese

1 pear, sliced lengthwise then cut into 1/4-inch strips

12 curly endive leaves

1/2 cup Balsamic Sauce (page 141)

1 On the rolling mat, arrange 2 double-layer slices of prosciutto to form about a 5 x 7-inch wrapper.

2 Wet your hands and spread about 1/2 cup Sushi Rice evenly over the prosciutto, leaving a 1-inch border at the top. Sprinkle about 2 teaspoons Gorgonzola in a horizontal line across the middle of the rice.

3 Place 2 pairs of pear strips end to end next to the Gorgonzola. Place 2 or 3 endive leaves in a line next to the nearest side of the pears, allowing the leaves to protrude from the ends.

4 Roll up according to the Small Roll method (page 25). Serve with Balsamic Sauce for dipping.

VARIATIONS Instead of using pears, grill 3 Mission figs brushed with port and dusted with brown sugar. Also try using thin ham slices as the outside wrapper, and thin Havarti cheese and apple slices as the filling.

elvis roll

Many a lip curls at the sound of this roll: "Ew! That sounds just plain wrong!" I myself was a sneering skeptic until I tried it and, well, the King describes it best: "Oh, baby, baby." This roll has to be tasted to be believed. Find egg roll wrappers in your supermarket's refrigerated section, usually next to the tofu.

MAKES 4 WRAPPED TEMPURA ROLLS

4 square sheets egg or spring roll wrappers

1½ cups prepared Sushi Rice (page 18)

4 to 6 teaspoons peanut butter

4 fried bacon slices, trimmed to 5½ x ½-inch strips

1 banana, quartered lengthwise and trimmed into 4-inch strips

5 cups canola or peanut oil, for frying

Basic Tempura Batter (page 44)

½ cup soy sauce, for dipping

Mayonnaise, for dipping

1 Angle a wrapper on a work surface with a corner tip pointing toward you. Wet your hands and scoop out 2 to 2½ tablespoons of rice and spread it in a horizontal rectangle shape in the middle of the wrapper.

2 Dab 1 teaspoon peanut butter in a horizontal line across the middle of the rice. Place 1 bacon strip (cut the bacon in half lengthwise if it is thicker than ½ inch) on top of the peanut butter. Place 1 banana strip alongside the bacon. Keep the ends of the roll neat. Fold up the bottom end point of the wrapper over the ingredients. Fold in the 2 side flaps, then roll forward to close the roll.

3 In a heavy pot, heat the oil to 350°F. Dip the roll into the batter and then slide carefully into the oil. Fry the roll for about 1 minute, until golden brown, turning once. Remove the roll to a cutting board.

4 Without wetting your knife, cut the roll into 4 or 6 even pieces. Serve immediately with soy sauce and a side of mayonnaise for dipping.

rambo bowl

This manly man's meal is a simple yet hearty bowl of stir-fried steak and scallions. For the really robust, throw in a handful of provolone or mozzarella cheese and get an instant Philly steak–like groove.

MAKES 4 SERVINGS

1 cup beef broth

½ cup soy sauce

1 tablespoon mirin

3 tablespoons sugar

¼ teaspoon onion powder

1½ to 2 pounds (1-inch-thick) sirloin

2 teaspoons olive oil

2 tablespoons canola or peanut oil

6 scallions, trimmed and cut into 2-inch pieces, plus 1 scallion cut into thin rings for garnish

½ cup shredded mozzarella or provolone cheese (optional)

4 cups prepared Sushi Rice (page 18)

Chili paste (optional)

1 In a small saucepan, combine the broth, soy sauce, mirin, sugar, and onion powder. Stir over low heat until the sugar dissolves. Remove from the heat and set aside.

2 Place the steak in a shallow dish and pour ½ cup of the soy sauce mixture and the olive oil over the steaks. Let marinate for about 30 minutes. Remove the steak from the marinade and thinly slice. Reserve the marinade.

3 In a large skillet, heat the canola oil over medium-high heat. Stir-fry the scallions for about 2 minutes. Add the sliced beef and 1 tablespoon of the marinade and fry for about 1 minute, until the meat just loses its redness. Turn off the heat and add the cheese if you like; cover to let the cheese melt, about 1 minute.

4 Divide the warm rice among 4 serving bowls and cover with 4 equal portions of scallion and beef. Garnish with the scallion rings. Serve with the remaining sauce and a side of chili paste, if desired.

NOTE To make the sauce thicker, add 2 teaspoons of cornstarch dissolved in a little water to the sauce remaining in the pot. Bring to a gentle boil, stirring constantly, for 1 minute. Set aside until serving.

VARIATION Add extra vegetables to the scallion-fry, like carrots, celery, broccoli, and cabbage.

ginger tuna bowl

The Japanese use an herb called shiso *for many of their dishes to invoke a clean, green taste to food. The closest we can get to the taste of shiso is in this salad's combination of basil and mint. This is a gorgeous salad, dewy and gently dressed with fresh ginger and soy sauce.*

MAKES 4 SERVINGS

1 tablespoon canola
or peanut oil

1½ pounds very fresh ahi or
albacore tuna steaks

MARINADE

6 tablespoons soy sauce

4 teaspoons sugar

1 tablespoon grated fresh ginger

4 tablespoons toasted white sesame seeds

4 cups prepared Sushi Rice (page 18)

GARNISHES

2 tablespoons julienned fresh basil

1 tablespoon julienned fresh mint

1 (2-inch) piece peeled fresh ginger,
cut into thin matchsticks

½ cup soy sauce,
for serving

1 In a medium skillet, heat the oil over high heat. Sear the tuna steaks for 30 seconds on each side. Place the tuna steaks on a cutting board and slice crosswise in ¼-inch slices.

2 In a glass baking dish, place the tuna slices in a single layer. In a small saucepan, combine the soy sauce, sugar, and ginger and bring just to a boil. Remove from the heat and let cool. Pour the marinade over the tuna and let marinate for 15 minutes in the refrigerator.

3 In a small sauté pan, toast the sesame seeds over medium heat until the seeds get glossy and fragrant. (Do this even if they are pretoasted; it freshens the taste.) Mix the sesame seeds into the Sushi Rice. Divide the rice equally among 4 bowls. Top each rice bowl with one quarter of the marinated tuna and some marinade sauce.

4 Toss the basil and mint strips together and garnish each of the bowls. Top each bowl with a few ginger matchsticks. Serve with soy sauce on the side.

five happiness rice

This is a sushi Crock-Pot dish. All the ingredients cook together in the rice cooker, so when the rice is done, dinner is ready! This warm sushi comfort food is accented by your choice of any or all of the crisp, raw garnishes.

MAKES 4 TO 6 SERVINGS

1 In the rice cooker insert, combine the rice, chicken, and vegetables. Combine the broth and soy sauce and pour over the rice mixture. Do not stir.

2 Turn the cooker on and cook as usual. Be sure to let the rice sit, undisturbed, for 15 minutes after the cooker turns off the Cook setting.

3 Top each bowl with your choice of garnishes. Sprinkle each serving with sesame-salt seasoning. Serve with soy sauce.

VARIATIONS Substitute precooked leeks, green beans, turnips, or potatoes, along with duck or slightly precooked pork.

3 cups short-grain rice, washed and dried for 30 minutes

½ cup boneless chicken, cut into 1-inch chunks

1 carrot, peeled and coarsely chopped

½ cup coarsely chopped onion

½ cup coarsely chopped brown shiitake or cremini mushrooms

1 cup chopped spinach or mustard greens

4 cups chicken broth

¼ cup soy sauce

GARNISHES

Chopped red radish

Chopped scallion

Fresh bean sprouts

Crushed peanuts

Sesame-salt seasoning (page 15)

½ cup plain soy sauce or any flavored soy sauce

sushi mosaic salad

A veritable Mondrian of a sushi salad, this can be made with short-grain brown rice or white sushi rice. Use the small Japanese pumpkins called kabocha if you can find them, or use very small pumpkins or medium-sized acorn squash instead. Their shells make lovely serving bowls, or serve the salad in double-layered lettuce leaves. Use all or some of the vegetables listed, or come up with your own combination.

MAKES 4 SERVINGS

4 small pumpkins or acorn squash, halved, seeds reserved

4 teaspoons peanut or canola oil

1½ teaspoons seasoned salt

½ teaspoon sugar

2 tablespoons finely chopped carrots, blanched

2 tablespoons finely chopped red bell pepper

2 tablespoons finely chopped yellow bell pepper

2 tablespoons finely chopped red onion

2 tablespoons finely chopped shiitake or brown mushrooms

2 tablespoons shelled and cooked soybeans (edamame) or cooked green peas

2 tablespoons finely chopped broccoli florets, blanched

4 cups cooked brown or white Sushi Rice (page 18)

8 large green leaf lettuce leaves, double layered to make 4 "bowls" (optional)

1 Preheat the oven to 325°F. Cut the pumpkin or squash three quarters of the way up to yield a bottom and a top. With a large serving spoon, scrape the seeds and pulp out of the bottom halves; reserve the seeds. Take the bottoms and tops of the pumpkin or squash, place in a large baking dish, and bake for 20 minutes, until tender. Let cool. Leave the oven on to roast the seeds.

2 To make seasoned pumpkin seeds: Wash the pulp from the seeds and pat dry with paper towels. In a small mixing bowl, coat the seeds with the oil. Mix the salt and sugar with the seeds. On a large cookie sheet, spread the seeds out in a single layer. Bake the seeds for 20 to 30 minutes, stirring a few times, until they are a rich golden brown.

3 In a large mixing bowl, gently fold all of the vegetables (except the lettuce) into the Sushi Rice.

4 Fill each bottom shell (or lettuce leaves) with the rice mixture. Sprinkle with the seeds and top with your choice of garnishes. Serve with a small pitcher of Citrus Soy Dipping Sauce or Ginger Soy Dipping Sauce.

GARNISHES

Roasted pumpkin seeds (see step 2)

4 radishes, cut into wafer-thin slices

Cilantro or parsley sprigs

4 teaspoons chopped chives

½ cup Citrus Soy Dipping Sauce (page 141) or Ginger Soy Dipping Sauce (page 140)

sweet

sushi

Sushi can be sweet and pretty to eat—just dress your rice with sweet pudding instead of *sushi-zu*. With just one master recipe for sweet sushi rice, you can change the taste with different pudding flavors and other accents. Make sure to dress the rice while it's still warm so it will absorb the dressing better. Sweet sushi rice requires a lot more dressing than regular Sushi Rice, but never fear—even though it will appear runny at first, the rice will absorb the sweet dressing.

sushi-rice pudding

Here's how to turn your sushi rice into a sweet treat with pudding mix, cream cheese, and whipped cream. Real, freshly whipped cream is best.

DRESSES 3 CUPS COOKED RICE

1 small (7-gram) envelope plain gelatin powder dissolved in 2 tablespoons hot water

1 cup warm prepared vanilla pudding

1 teaspoon vanilla extract

½ cup mascarpone or cream cheese, cut into bits and softened at room temperature

½ cup heavy cream, whipped with 2 tablespoons sugar, or substitute Cool Whip

3 cups cooked, undressed Sushi Rice (page 18)

1 Stir the dissolved gelatin into the pudding. Stir in the extract.

2 Mix in the mascarpone or cream cheese. Fold in the whipped cream or Cool Whip. Dress the warm rice with the pudding.

3 Refrigerate the sweet rice for 1 hour to set.

butterscotch scoops

Serve these sweet and crunchy scoops in rainbow-colored ice cream cones.

MAKES 8 CONES

1 Mix the Buttershots liqueur and 5 tablespoons toffee bits into the butterscotch pudding. Dress the warm sushi rice with the pudding mixture. Refrigerate the bowl to let the sweet rice set for 1 hour.

2 Wet your hands and scoop out about ½ cup rice and form into a ball. Set the ball on a sheet of wax paper. Continue this process until you have 8 evenly formed balls. (The rice balls can be made up to this point a day ahead.)

3 Spread the remaining ⅓ cup toffee bits evenly on a large plate. Dip the top half of the rice ball into the toffee bits to coat.

¼ cup
Buttershots liqueur

**5 tablespoons plus
⅓ cup Heath Almond
Toffee Bits**

**1 cup prepared
butterscotch pudding**

**3 cups cooked,
undressed Sushi Rice
(page 18)**

**8 ice cream
cones**

4 Holding a rice ball in your palm, topping-side down, gently fit the opening of the cone onto the rice ball. Turn the ball and the cone upright and secure the bottom edge to the cone, reshaping the rice ball. Continue with the remaining 7 rice balls.

5 To serve, wrap the cones in colorful cocktail napkins and set in champagne flutes or other slender glasses.

sushi crispies

These "treats" almost look like real sushi pieces, but real sushi was never this sweet and peanut buttery.

MAKES ABOUT 24 BARS

3 tablespoons butter

7½ cups Rice Krispies cereal

1 (16-ounce) bag regular marshmallows

⅓ cup smooth peanut butter

¼ cup prepared hot fudge sauce

1 Butter an (8-inch-square) glass baking dish. Prepare Rice Krispies Treats according to the instructions on the box. Spread into the baking dish, pressing firmly to flatten to ¼-inch thickness. Reserve the leftover marshmallows for toppings.

2 When the Rice Krispies Treats have cooled, remove both from the dishes in flat pieces to a large cutting board. Wet a knife blade and cut the Rice Krispies Treats into 1-inch-wide strips. Turn each strip onto its side, wet the knife blade, and split each strip lengthwise in two.

3 Spread each strip half with a thin layer of peanut butter and sandwich the strips back together. Wet the knife blade and cut each sandwich crosswise into approximately 2½-inch bars (about 3 bars per strip).

4 With scissors, cut each marshmallow lengthwise into 3 even pieces. Place a piece of marshmallow on top of each rice bar. Put as many bars as will fit without touching on microwavable plates and set aside.

5 Spoon the hot fudge sauce into a small sandwich bag and microwave for 10 seconds, until the sauce is warm. Snip a tiny hole in a corner of the bag. Hold like a pastry bag and squeeze a ¼-inch-wide bar of fudge sauce across the middle of the marshmallow and Rice Krispies Treat piece.

6 Place the rice bars in the microwave and heat on Medium for 5 to 20 seconds, until the marshmallows are soft.

SEE PHOTOGRAPH ON PAGE 124

key lime cups

These tangy tropical tartlets are a great twist on Key lime pie—
sweet rice dressed with rum and Key lime zest syrup.

MAKES 15 CUPS

**15 frozen
mini–phyllo dough cups**

SWEET RICE

½ cup sugar

**½ cup fresh or bottled
Key lime juice**

Grated zest of 2 Key limes

3 tablespoons light rum

**1 cup cooked, undressed
Sushi Rice (page 18)**

FILLING

3 eggs, at room temperature

**½ cup fresh or bottled
Key lime juice**

**1 (14-ounce) can sweetened
condensed milk**

**1 teaspoon
cream of tartar**

1 Preheat the oven to 350°F. Arrange the phyllo cups on a baking sheet and heat them for 3 to 5 minutes to crisp. Set aside to cool.

2 In a small saucepan, mix the sugar, lime juice, lime zest, and 1 cup of water. Bring to a boil. Remove from the heat and stir in the rum. Dress the Sushi Rice with the warm lime-rum syrup and set aside.

3 For the filling, separate the eggs, putting the yolks into a medium mixing bowl and the whites into a large mixing bowl. Set the whites aside. Whisk the egg yolks briefly, then whisk in the ½ cup lime juice. Stir the condensed milk into the egg mixture and set aside.

4 Beat the egg whites to soft peaks and gradually add the cream of tartar. Continue beating until the egg whites reach stiff peaks. Fold the milk mixture into the egg whites. Chill the filling mixture for 1 hour before using. (The filling mixture will keep for 24 hours in an airtight container in the refrigerator.)

5 Scoop out 2 teaspoons sweet rice and press lightly into each pastry cup. Top with about 2 teaspoons filling. Serve immediately or store in the refrigerator for up to 3 hours. Allow cups to soften at room temperature for 15 minutes before serving.

fruiti sushi

This delicious fruit sushi is a delight to see and to eat. Let your imagination help you create an array of shapes and colors with lovely layers of fruit. You will be cutting shapes out of the fruit slices with the cookie cutters. For the mango slices, I cut down the flat sides lengthwise, around the pit, and right through the skin. Then just trim the skin away from each slice. It's easier, and there's no wrestling with a slippery mango.

MAKES 22 PIECES

2 tablespoons finely grated unsweetened coconut

3 tablespoons Malibu liqueur, or other coconut-flavored liqueur

3 cups Sushi-Rice Pudding (page 126), made with coconut pudding instead of vanilla

1 mango, cut lengthwise into ⅛-inch slices

4 honeydew melon slices, cut lengthwise into ⅛-inch-thick slices

4 cantaloupe melon slices, cut lengthwise into ⅛-inch-thick slices

2 kiwifruit, cut crosswise into ⅛-inch-thick circles

5 to 6 strawberries, cut crosswise into ⅛-inch-thick slices

2 to 3 small starfruit, cut diagonally in ⅛-inch slices (optional), or 8 to 10 green grapes, cut crosswise into circles

1 Line the bottom and sides of a 13 x 9-inch glass baking dish with wax paper, allowing a 2-inch overhang.

2 Fold the grated coconut and Malibu liqueur into the whipped cream and then into the Sushi-Rice Pudding.

3 Spread the rice pudding into the baking dish to a ¼-inch thickness. Smooth the top with a damp rubber spatula. (You may have a little leftover rice.) Refrigerate until the sweet rice is set, about 1 hour.

4 Dip a 2¼-inch cookie cutter in cold water and shake off the excess water. Cut shapes out of the rice, starting at the edges of the dish. Pull up wax paper to get underneath the rice and push up the shaped rice through the cutter to remove. Set aside on a large platter. Continue cutting

RECIPE CONTINUES

SUGAR GLAZE

½ cup sugar

1 tablespoon cornstarch

1 cup cold water

1 teaspoon lemon extract

GARNISHES

Blueberries

Raspberries

1 tablespoon lime zest

1 tablespoon orange zest

1 tablespoon lemon zest

Mint leaves

until all of the rice is used. Use assorted 2-inch cookie cutters to cut shapes out of the mango and melons. Use 1-inch cookie cutters to cut the kiwis and strawberries in an assortment of shapes.

5 Stack large fruit slices on top of the matching rice shapes. Stack small fruit slices for the second layer. Stack a starfruit slice or grape circle for the third layer.

6 To glaze the stacks, mix the first 3 ingredients for the sugar glaze in a small saucepan and heat slowly, stirring until the sugar is dissolved and the mixture turns clear. Remove from the heat and stir in the lemon extract. Brush or spoon the glaze over the sushi pieces and allow to set. Top with a blueberry or a raspberry, a few zest curls, and mint leaves.

pastel delights

These beautiful rolls are wrapped up in rice wrappers dyed with tender pastel colors. The sweet rice recipe is flavored with pineapple Jell-O and crushed pineapple instead of pudding. Be sure to have extra rice wrappers on hand, since these delicate sheets take patience to handle.

MAKES 6 ROLLS

1 Drain the canned pineapple, reserving all of the juice. Prepare the Jell-O according to package directions, using the reserved pineapple juice as part of the 2 cups water. Remove the Jell-O from the heat.

2 Add the mascarpone and mix until smooth. Add the vanilla extract to the whipped cream, and add the Jell-O mixture to the whipped cream. Fold the Sushi Rice into the Jell-O mixture. Stir in the crushed pineapple. Do not refrigerate the rice. Cover with a damp towel and keep standing by.

3 Cover a cutting board with a sheet of wax or parchment paper. Cut the honeydew, cantaloupe, and pineapple into 4 x 4¼-inch sticks on the paper, and use the paper to transfer the juices to a small bowl. Place the fruit sticks in individual dishes. Mix the honey with the reserved fruit juices and set aside.

½ small (3.2-ounce) can crushed pineapple, with juice

1 (3-ounce) package pineapple Jell-O

4 ounces mascarpone or cream cheese, softened at room temperature and cut into bits

1 teaspoon vanilla extract

½ cup freshly whipped heavy cream with 3 tablespoons sugar or Cool Whip

3 cups cooked, undressed Sushi Rice (page 18)

¼ small honeydew melon

¼ small cantaloupe melon

¼ small pineapple

3 tablespoons honey, liquefied in a microwave for 10 seconds

Assorted food colorings

1 package 6½-inch-square rice stick wrappers

1 bunch of mint

RECIPE CONTINUES

4 Into a dish or skillet big enough to accommodate the rice wrappers without their edges curling up, pour 1 cup of hot (not boiling) water. Add 4 to 5 drops of a single food coloring and mix well. Take a sheet of rice wrapper and immerse it in the colored water for about 20 seconds, or until the edges begin to curl up. For stronger wrapper power, double the layers but soak one at a time. Carefully remove the wrapper from the water and place it flat on a large cutting board. Do not pat it dry. Repeat the process with 2 or 3 additional colors, keeping the colored wrappers separate.

5 Spread about 1/2 cup sweet rice on a wrapper, leaving a 1-inch border on the bottom and sides and a 2-inch border at the top.

6 Place 2 pairs of each fruit in a line across the lower quarter of rice. Place 2 mint sprigs on either end of the roll.

7 Carefully roll the wrapper up and around the filling. Try to keep it as tight as possible without tearing the rice wrapper. (This is where the patience part kicks in.) Set the roll aside, laying on the seam to set. Continue the process with the remaining 5 rolls. The rolls can be covered with barely damp paper towels and plastic wrap and refrigerated for up to 30 minutes.

8 Cut the rolls into 4 even pieces like regular sushi rolls. Garnish the plates with mint leaves and serve with the honey dipping sauce.

VARIATIONS Substitute other flavored Jell-Os, like lemon, apricot, strawberry, or raspberry. The pineapple accent in the rice works well with all of these.

chunky monkey roll

Yes! We do have bananas! Walnut chunks and deep chocolate bits enrich the banana ice cream wrapped in banana rice. Add your favorite chocolate sauce and go ape.

MAKES 8 OR 10 ROLLS

4 cups canola or peanut oil, for frying

1 (7-gram) envelope plain gelatin powder, dissolved in 2 tablespoons cold water

1 teaspoon vanilla extract

1 cup prepared banana pudding

4 ounces mascarpone or cream cheese, cut into bits and softened at room temperature

3 cups cooked, undressed Sushi Rice (page 18)

1 package 6-inch-square roll wrappers

1 pint Ben & Jerry's Chunky Monkey ice cream

Basic Tempura Batter (page 44)

Prepared chocolate syrup

1 Heat the oil in a large heavy-bottomed pot over medium heat to 340°F.

2 Meanwhile, stir the dissolved gelatin and vanilla extract into the pudding. Mix in the mascarpone.

3 Mix the Sushi Rice into the pudding mixture to dress. Set aside.

4 Angle an egg roll wrapper on a work surface with a corner tip pointing toward you. Wet your hands, scoop out ¼ cup of rice, and spread in a horizontal rectangle shape in the middle of the wrapper.

5 Working quickly, use a tablespoon to scoop out 4 tablespoons ice cream, arranging them horizontally in the middle of the rice. Fold the bottom point of the wrapper over the fillings. Fold in the side flaps toward the center, like an envelope. Continue rolling forward to close the roll. Moisten the top edges with water to seal.

6 Dip the roll into tempura batter to coat, then slide carefully into the hot oil. Fry for about 1 minute, or until the batter is golden brown. With tongs, remove from the oil and place onto a cutting board.

7 Cut into 2 or 4 even pieces. Squeeze swirls of chocolate syrup over each cut roll and serve immediately. Repeat with the remaining rolls.

sauces

and

mayonnaises

Sauces are the last layer of flavor and the final spike of taste in savory sushi dishes. Use these simple sauces for dipping rolls, dressing sushi salads, and marinating. Mayonnaises are added directly into sushi rolls and/or can be offered as a side dish for a bonus dipping indulgence. Keep your flavored soy sauces and mayonnaises refrigerated in glass screw-top jars or plastic squeeze bottles.

jalapeño soy dipping sauce

MAKES 1 CUP

1 cup
soy sauce

1 jalapeño, thinly
sliced crosswise

Combine the ingredients in a glass jar. Shake well. Refrigerate and keep up to 4 weeks.

NOTE The flavor will get hotter with age. Remove the pepper slices when the desired potency is reached.

ginger soy dipping sauce

MAKES 1 CUP

Measure the soy sauce into a screw-top glass jar. Using the edge of a regular teaspoon, scrape the skin off of the ginger knob. Grate the peeled ginger on a ginger grater or the small round holes of a regular grater. Gather the pulp and squeeze the juice into the soy sauce. Close the jar and shake well. Refrigerate and keep up to 4 weeks.

1 cup soy sauce

4-inch knob of
fresh ginger

tempura dipping sauce

½ cup soy sauce

2 teaspoons rice wine
vinegar or lemon juice

2 teaspoons mirin
or 1 teaspoon sugar
in 1 teaspoon
white wine

MAKES ABOUT ¾ CUP

In a small saucepan, combine the soy sauce, ⅓ cup water, vinegar, and mirin and bring to a boil. Immediately remove from the heat and let cool. Tempura sauce is best when used fresh, but it will keep refrigerated for a few days.

citrus soy dipping sauce

MAKES ABOUT 1¼ CUPS

¾ **cup soy sauce**

5 tablespoons lemon juice, strained

3 teaspoons orange juice, strained

Combine the ingredients in a glass jar. Shake well. Refrigerate and keep up to 4 weeks.

sesame soy sauce

MAKES ABOUT 1 CUP

1 cup soy sauce

2 teaspoons pure sesame oil

2 teaspoons toasted white sesame seeds

Combine the ingredients in a screw-top glass jar. Shake well. Refrigerate and keep up to 4 weeks. Bring to room temperature before using and shake well to mix the oil and soy sauce.

balsamic sauce

MAKES ABOUT ¾ CUP

1 cup balsamic vinegar

1 tablespoon brown sugar

1 tablespoon butter

1 tablespoon Worcestershire sauce

1 tablespoon fig jam or puréed fig preserves

In a saucepan, bring the vinegar to a boil, then reduce the heat and simmer, uncovered, for 10 minutes. The vinegar should reduce its volume by half and become syrupy. Stir in the brown sugar, butter, Worcestershire sauce, and fig jam and simmer for another 5 minutes. Remove from the heat and strain through a fine-mesh sieve if seeds are present. Let cool.

Balsamic Sauce will keep refrigerated in a glass screw-top jar for weeks. The flavor will become smoother with time.

Before using the chilled sauce, remove the top and microwave the sauce for about 20 seconds to melt the butter. Replace the top and shake well.

lemon mayonnaise

MAKES ¾ CUP

½ cup mayonnaise

1 tablespoon sour cream

½ teaspoon finely grated lemon zest (from about ½ lemon)

5 teaspoons fresh lemon juice

In a small glass mixing bowl, combine all the ingredients.

spicy mayonnaise

MAKES ½ CUP

½ cup mayonnaise

1 teaspoon Sriracha chili sauce

In a small bowl, mix the ingredients with a fork to combine well. Add more chili sauce for more fire.

wasabi mayonnaise

MAKES ½ CUP

½ cup mayonnaise

2 teaspoons wasabi powder mixed with a few drops of water or 2 teaspoons wasabi paste

In a small bowl, mix the ingredients well.

index